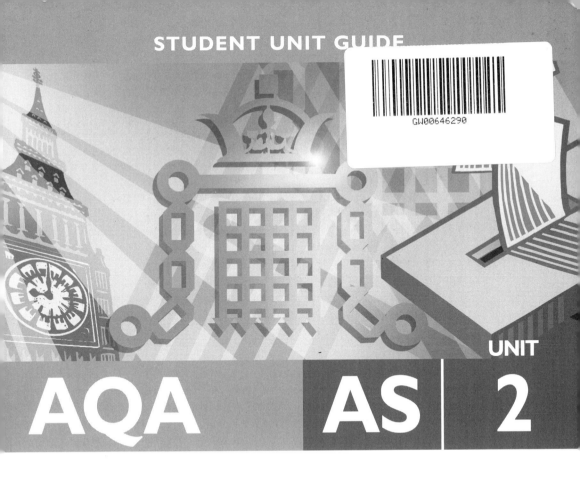

AQA AS | UNIT 2

Government & Politics

Governing Modern Britain

Paul Fairclough

Philip Allan Updates, an imprint of Hodder Education, part of Hachette Livre UK, Market Place, Deddington, Oxfordshire OX15 0SE

Orders

Bookpoint Ltd, 130 Milton Park, Abingdon, Oxfordshire, OX14 4SB
tel: 01235 827720
fax: 01235 400454
e-mail: uk.orders@bookpoint.co.uk
Lines are open 9.00 a.m.–5.00 p.m., Monday to Saturday, with a 24-hour message answering service. You can also order through the Philip Allan Updates website: www.philipallan.co.uk

ISBN 978-0-340-95958-9

First printed 2008
Impression number 5 4 3 2 1
Year 2013 2012 2011 2010 2009 2008

This guide has been written specifically to support students preparing for the AQA AS Government & Politics Unit 2 examination. The content has been neither approved nor endorsed by AQA and remains the sole responsibility of the author.

Typeset by Phoenix Photosetting, Chatham, Kent
Printed by MPG Books Ltd, Bodmin

Hachette Livre UK's policy is to use papers that are natural, renewable and recyclable products and made from wood grown in sustainable forests. The logging and manufacturing processes are expected to conform to the environmental regulations of the country of origin.

Contents

Introduction

■ ■ ■

Content Guidance

■ ■ ■

Questions and Answers

Introduction

The AQA Advanced Subsidiary (AS) in Government & Politics, taught for the first time from September 2008, is a two-unit course. This guide has been written as a companion for students taking Unit 2 Governing Modern Britain. It aims to provide a clear outline of the way in which the unit is structured and examined, as well as providing students with a summary of the core content for each part of the unit. The first unit of the new AS, People, Politics and Participation, is the subject of a separate unit guide.

The specification (i.e. the syllabus) content for Unit 2 is divided into four broad areas:

(1) The British constitution: the nature and sources of the British constitution and the part played by the senior judiciary — both traditionally and in the light of recent developments, e.g. UK membership of the EU and the passage of the Human Rights Act (1998).

(2) Parliament: the main roles and functions of Parliament and the way in which they are discharged by the House of Commons and the Lords; the principle of parliamentary sovereignty and the extent to which Parliament is able to hold the government to account.

(3) The core executive: the main individuals and bodies that comprise the core executive and how they relate to one another; where power resides within the core executive, in particular the ever-changing relationships between the prime minister, cabinet and the bureaucracy.

(4) Multi-level governance: the main elements of government at sub-national and supra-national level; their significance and how such bodies relate to the government at Westminster; specifically, looks at elected local and devolved institutions and the main institutions of the European Union.

How to use this guide

The guide is divided into three sections.

- This **Introduction** outlines the aims of the guide, provides a general overview of the unit, offers some initial thoughts regarding assessment, considers the skills required to succeed in the subject, and gives advice regarding approaches to revision and the exam.
- The **Content Guidance** section addresses the key elements of the unit content more systematically, providing a summary of the core content of which candidates must be able to demonstrate a good knowledge and understanding. For ease of reference, the various headings in this section mirror those in the specification.
- The **Questions and Answers** section contains a range of AS Unit 2-style questions, along with model answers of varying length and quality. The examiner comments that accompany these answers will help students understand precisely what the examiners are looking for.

The specification at a glance

Unit 2 focuses on the institutions of government at sub-national, national and European level. The more 'political' aspects of the course are dealt with in Unit 1. The main themes of Unit 2 are, therefore, power and decision-making — how government is organised and how the various institutions of government relate to one another. The specification clearly identifies the main debates, the key concepts and the content that relate to each of the four areas listed on p. 4. These are given in the tables below.

The British constitution

Issues, debates and processes to be addressed	Key concepts	Content and amplification
The nature and sources of the British constitution	• Written/unwritten • Codified/uncodified • Unitary/federal • Rigid/flexible	• A knowledge of the main sources of the British constitution: statute case law, conventions, treaties, constitutional change • How far the British constitution influences and limits the powers of government
The judiciary and its relationship to other 'powers' of government	• Judicial independence • Separation of powers • Judicial review	• The relationship of the judiciary to the executive and legislature • Judicial appointments • The impact of the Human Rights Act and the European Court of Human Rights upon the British political system

Parliament

Issues, debates and processes to be addressed	Key concepts	Content and amplification
The role of Parliament in the UK's political system	• Representation • Parliamentary sovereignty • Mandate	• The composition and main roles and functions of Parliament: representation, legislation, scrutiny • The relative powers of the House of Commons and the House of Lords • Parliamentary sovereignty in theory and practice
Parliament and government relationships	• Accountability • Executive dominance • Elective dictatorship • Bicameral	• The roles of the House of Commons and House of Lords in scrutinising legislation and holding the government to account • The influence of backbenchers, frontbenchers, whips and the opposition

The core executive

Issues, debates and processes to be addressed	Key concepts	Content and amplification
Relations within the core executive The prime minister and the cabinet system	• Prime ministerial and cabinet government • Presidentialism • Collective responsibility	• The prime minister: main roles, powers and resources • The cabinet system: composition, roles and functions of cabinet, cabinet committees and cabinet ministers • The Cabinet Office • Prime ministerial and presidential systems: a brief comparison • Do we have prime ministerial government in Britain?
Policy-making and implementation	• Bureaucracy • Political neutrality • Anonymity • Permanence • Individual ministerial responsibility	• Ministers and civil servants: main characteristics, roles, resources and relationships • Special advisers • Government departments

Multi-level governance

Issues, debates and processes to be addressed	Key concepts	Content and amplification
Elected local and devolved government in the UK	• Elected representatives • Local democracy • Devolution	• The main powers of elected local government, the Scottish Parliament and Welsh Assembly • Relations between the Westminster Parliament and elected local and devolved government • Debates on the nature and extent of devolved power
The European Union	• Supra-national • 'Democratic deficit'	• The composition and main powers of the European Parliament, the European Council and Council of Ministers, and the Commission • Where does power lie? Is there a 'democratic deficit'? • The impact of EU institutions on the Westminster Parliament

Revision planning

Revision is personal and the way in which you revise will be guided largely by what works for you. That said, there are a number of points you need to take on board at an early stage if you are aiming for a top grade.

First, it is important that you familiarise yourself with the main elements of the AQA specification, i.e. the Unit 2 content and the format of the examination. Specifically, you should know:

- how the unit content is divided between different sections
- precisely what you do and do not need to know in each section
- the number of questions on each paper
- how these questions relate to the sections in the unit content (e.g. one question per section of content — or a random number?)
- how much choice you will have on the Unit 2 paper (i.e. are there any compulsory questions or compulsory sections?)
- the type of questions you will face

All of this information is provided later on in this guide, though it may also be helpful for you to get hold of your own copy of the full AQA Government & Politics specification. If your teacher has not already given you this document at the start of the course your first port of call should be the AQA website (**www.aqa.org.uk**), where you will find a downloadable PDF of the full specification along with sample examination papers and other useful material. These sample papers will enable you to familiarise yourself with the range and mix of questions you are likely to face in the real examination. They will also give you the chance to see the advice and the rules (or 'rubrics') that accompany the questions on the paper.

Five steps to effective revision

(1) As already mentioned, the first thing you need to do is get hold of the full AQA subject specification (syllabus), a selection of specimen papers or past papers, and any other available guidance. Make sure that all of the material you collect relates to the new 2008 specification rather than the old 'legacy' course. If in doubt, remember that the title of the old AQA Unit 2 ('GOV2 Parties, Pressure Groups and Protest Movements') is different from that of the new Unit 2 ('GOVP2 Governing Modern Britain'). Note that the format of questions has changed too: the old Unit 2 papers consisted entirely of two-part questions, whereas the new Unit 2 questions are all three-part.

(2) You will need to work out a realistic revision timetable. This should incorporate all of your subjects and be broken down into focused sessions of around 40 minutes, divided by breaks. These breaks are important. If you leave no time for relaxation your revision will be less effective and you will be less likely to keep to your timetable.

(3) Using the content summary from this guide, or the specification itself, go through your folder and divide up your notes between the four broad content areas identified. It might help you to photocopy the 'paragraph' of the specification that relates to each section of the unit content, and then put these sheets on top of each pile of notes. Alternatively, you could use subject dividers labelled with the various Unit 2 section headings as a means of organising your notes. When this is done you should have several piles of notes — each one relating to a single topic — or one or more lever-arch files, divided and indexed in line with the specification content.

(4) The next task is to check your notes and make sure that you have covered all of the items on the specification. Look through each pile of notes, checking off each topic against the content summary from the specification and the core content provided in this guide. Are there big gaps? It may be that you have mislaid some notes — or that you missed some lessons and failed to catch up. It is also possible that your teacher has left out certain sections for a good reason: perhaps a lack of time if you are being entered for the Unit 2 examination in the January of year 12. Check it out. Make sure that you are not missing something vital. If you find that there are gaps, you need to work quickly. If the exam is still some way off, you may have time to reinforce any particularly thin topics by expanding the outline notes provided in the Content Guidance section, by copying up notes from friends, or by undertaking some background reading of your own. If the problem is largely down to a lack of understanding — rather than a lack of notes — you may be able to seek individual help from your teacher.

If the examination is only a few weeks away, however, something more drastic is probably called for. This guide is aimed at helping you to familiarise yourself with the scope and demands of Unit 2. Though the Content Guidance section will point you in the right direction, you will need to look elsewhere for greater depth. There are, however, a number of books on the market that provide the kind of factual summaries that can help you to cut corners if time is short, e.g. Patrick Walsh-Atkins' *AS UK Government and Politics Exam Revision Notes* (Philip Allan Updates) or Paul Fairclough's *AS & A-level Government and Politics Through Diagrams* (Oxford University Press).

(5) Look at the specification content and the available specimen papers or past papers for each module. Which questions do you feel fairly confident about tackling? Which make you want to cry or retreat to your bed with a packet of custard creams? However tempting it is to start your revision with the topics you feel happy with, it really is better to grasp the nettle and address your weaknesses first. Once you have identified these weaker areas, you need to go through making summary notes. Try — if you can — to get each small topic onto a single page. This process of summarising should eventually leave you with a much less daunting set of memory-jogging revision notes. You could also try presenting your notes in different formats. Some books, for example, present the information in the form of diagrams. You could try turning these diagrams into prose or bullet points. Equally, try turning some of your own handwritten notes into diagrams. You will find that the very process of reformatting your notes in this way reinforces learning and develops a greater understanding of the material.

Five points to avoid

(1) Leaving your revision until it is too late. Though last-minute revision may have served you well at GCSE, students who adopt this approach at AS and A-level rarely come away with the kinds of grades of which they are capable. The depth of knowledge and understanding required at this level makes it difficult to use quick fixes.

(2) Staying at home when you should be attending in-school revision sessions. Though you may feel that you can do a better job yourself, the vast majority of students who adopt this approach do not achieve their potential. However pointless the school revision lessons may seem to you, they are probably helping you more than you realise.

(3) Revising for hours without a break or working for whole days on a single subject. A series of 40-minute sessions interspersed with 15-minute breaks can lead to more productive work. It is good to build some daily variety into your revision programme, by mixing and matching different subjects.

(4) Question spotting. Although it is recommended that you look at the kinds of questions that have turned up in the past, question spotting (i.e. trying to guess what the examiners will put on the exam paper) is a dangerous game. Even if your 'banker' topic does turn up, there is no guarantee that it is going to be phrased in such a way that you will want to tackle it.

(5) Leaving out major topics from your revision. This can be disastrous. I regularly mark examination scripts where candidates who are obviously able score a high A grade on one question and barely scrape a C grade on the other. The free choice of questions available in Unit 2 means that you will never be forced to answer a question, but failing to revise one or more of the four sections of unit content will seriously reduce your options if something really nasty appears on one of your preferred topics. It will also limit your overall ('synoptic') understanding of the subject. As is made clear in the specification:

Students must study all four sections of this unit. There are no optional topics within this unit. This unit will form the basis for later study and students will need to cover all topics as they may need to make reference to them in synoptic questions at A2.

Examinable skills

The Qualifications and Curriculum Authority (QCA) have identified the three assessment objectives (AOs) common to all three main Government & Politics specifications. At AS (i.e. Units 1 and 2), the assessment is weighted more towards AO1 (knowledge and understanding), whereas at A2 (i.e. Units 3 and 4), the emphasis shifts slightly, with 45% for AO1 and 35% for AO2 (analysis and evaluation). Though this shift clearly reflects the greater emphasis on analysis and evaluation required at A2, you will obviously need to do more at AS than simply demonstrate knowledge.

Assessment objectives		AS weighting
AO1	Demonstrate knowledge and understanding of relevant institutions, processes, political concepts, theories and debates	50%
AO2	Analyse and evaluate political information, arguments and explanations, and identify parallels, connections, similarities and differences between aspects of the political systems studied	30%
AO3	Construct and communicate coherent arguments making use of a range of appropriate political vocabulary	20%

Your AQA Unit 2 answers will be marked according to these assessment objectives. Examiners will not simply give you a mark out of 40 for each of the questions you tackle; marks will be available for each assessment objective, and the total mark for the question will therefore be arrived at by totalling the marks awarded for knowledge and understanding (AO1), analysis and evaluation (AO2) and communication (AO3) on each sub-question.

As we will see in the Questions and Answers section of this guide, there are four key elements to achieving a good mark when answering these questions:

(1) Take time to identify what the question is getting at — i.e. what you are being asked to do. Look for command words (e.g. discuss, analyse, evaluate, identify) and make sure that you do what is being asked of you.

(2) Try to write in an analytical (i.e. argument-led) style as opposed to simply describing. The latter may be rewarded on AO1, but you are unlikely to pick up many marks on AO2.

(3) Strike the right balance between theory and supporting examples. Ideally, each separate argument/point should be developed in a single paragraph and each point that you make should be supported by at least one example.

(4) Try to use appropriate political vocabulary. This will help you to score more highly on AO3.

As well as providing the outline assessment objectives for all A-level politics specifications, the QCA has also provided performance descriptors for answers at the A/B-grade boundary and the E/U-grade boundary. These descriptors (see below) are rather generic, but they do give you a good idea of what is required to achieve one of the top two grades.

Performance descriptors at AS

Grade	AO1	AO2	AO3
A/B boundary	Candidates characteristically: (a) demonstrate full and accurate knowledge of political institutions and processes and a sound understanding of political concepts, theories and debates (b) produce answers that deploy relevant knowledge to answer the question (c) demonstrate clear contextual awareness (d) use relevant evidence and, where appropriate, contemporary examples to illustrate points made	Candidates characteristically: (a) provide analyses that display a sound awareness of differing viewpoints and a clear recognition of issues (b) evaluate political institutions, processes and behaviour, applying appropriate concepts and theories (c) make valid comparisons	Candidates characteristically: (a) construct and communicate clear, structured and sustained arguments and explanations (b) use accurate political vocabulary
E/U boundary	Candidates characteristically: (a) demonstrate a basic knowledge of political institutions and processes and begin to show some understanding of political concepts, theories and debates (b) make a limited attempt at answering the question (c) produce at least one piece of relevant evidence, which may be drawn from source material provided	Candidates characteristically: (a) show some basic awareness of differing viewpoints (b) attempt simple evaluation of political institutions, processes and behaviour (c) make simple comparisons	Candidates characteristically: (a) attempt to communicate and develop an argument or explanation (b) use basic political vocabulary

On the examination day

Below are a few general points about how to maximise your chances in examinations once the revision is complete and the big day has finally arrived.

(1) Ensure that you know which topics/units are being examined on which day. This might sound obvious but it is not uncommon for candidates to miss examinations inadvertently, or to turn up having revised Latin Unit 2 only to find that they are in fact due to sit Politics Unit 2. It may be that you have an examination clash involving two or more subjects. If this is the case, make sure that you know which unit(s) you will be doing in the morning and which you will be sitting in the afternoon. It is your responsibility to make sure that you know which exam is on which day and whether exams are in the morning or afternoon. Even if you have revised for both subjects that are being examined on the same day, it can be unsettling to discover suddenly that you are tackling them in a different order from that which you had expected. These kinds of mistakes can cost grades.

(2) Make sure that you arrive in good time for the examination. If you arrive at the last minute, or even late, you will probably not be in the best frame of mind to tackle the examination paper. Arriving far too early can be just as bad if you are nervous by nature, as you may well manage to get yourself into a state before you even enter the examination room.

(3) Make sure that you arrive properly equipped. You should know what you need for the examination. Do not turn up without a pencil if you have spent your whole revision programme planning essays in pencil before you start. More importantly, think carefully about what pen you are going to use. Examiners frequently complain about the problems they have reading scripts written in scratchy and/or faint biro. It makes far more sense to use a black roller ball pen, a black gel pen or a black ink pen in examinations. Why lose valuable marks simply because your words of wisdom cannot be read?

(4) Timing is crucial. You must make a mental note of the total time available for the examination and the amount of time you have available to complete each question. It can be helpful to make a note of the times at which you should be starting each question or sub-question at the start of the examination. This will help you to make sure that you do not fall behind schedule. Remember, the number of extra marks that you will gain by spending a further 10 minutes on a question that you have already answered well will not make up for the marks that you lose as a result of only having 15 minutes left to do the last question. Be strict with yourself!

(5) Think carefully before you commit pen to paper. Although it can be tempting to start writing as soon as you open the question booklet, particularly if everyone else is scribbling away, it is far better to have a good look at all of the questions first to make sure that you haven't missed anything. It might be that the question on voting behaviour is there, after all, but it is just worded in a less obvious way. It would be a shame to miss your 'banker' topic as a result of your eagerness to start writing straightaway.

(6) Make sure that you do what is asked of you rather than simply writing what you want to write. If the question says 'explain' do not simply 'describe'. If it asks you to consider a particular period (e.g. the 1990s) then focus on that period rather than reeling off all of your examples from the 1960s.

(7) Strike the right balance between political theory and supporting examples. Answers that are overly theoretical, or those that simply describe recent events without any attempt to bring in theory, are likely to fail. Anyone can do the latter if they watch the news. You have been studying politics for at least a year and you should, therefore, be able to bring political theory into your evaluation of events, as well as putting those events into their historical context.

About the exam

Scheme of assessment

The switch from the old three-unit AS to the new two-unit model was accompanied by a 50% increase in the length of each AS unit examination — from 1 hour up to 1½ hours. Each of the two AS units (GOVP1 and GOVP2) now account for 50% of the total AS mark (25% of the overall A-level mark).

Exam format

AQA Unit 2 (GOVP2): Governing Modern Britain

Exam type	Written
Duration	1½ hours
Question choice	Candidates must answer any two questions from a choice of four
Question format	Each question consists of three parts (a, b and c) worth 5, 10 and 25 marks respectively. Each question is accompanied by a short piece of source material
Question focus	Each of the four questions on the exam paper will relate to one of the four sections of the specification content for the unit
Total marks available	80
Overall weighting	50% of the total AS marks (25% of the total A-level marks)

Timing

With each examination paper carrying a maximum of 80 marks and lasting 90 minutes, it is far easier to decide how much time to spend on each question than was once the case. Essentially, you should spend around 5 minutes on each part (a) question, 10 minutes on the part (b)s and around 25–30 minutes on the longer part (c) mini-essays.

Tackling the exam

Before you start writing

First, remember to scan through the whole paper before you start writing your first answer. It would be crazy to finish question 1 and get halfway through question 2 before you realised that your favourite topics had turned up on questions 3 and 4.

Second, make sure that you take time to read through all three parts of your chosen question before you commit yourself to taking it on. It is all too easy to waste time including irrelevant material in the 5-mark part (a) question, only to find that you are then required to write out the same material in parts (b) or (c). In an examination where every second is vital, you simply cannot afford to squander 2 or 3 minutes in this way.

The 5-mark part (a) questions

These questions ask you to explain a term or phrase used in the extract provided.

How to write an A-grade answer
- The first thing you need to do is provide a concise and unambiguous definition.
- Remember that this term is likely to be part of the vocabulary of politics. You should therefore be defining the term as it is used in the study of the subject, rather than just using a generic dictionary definition.
- Once you have provided your definition, you should use the material in the extract and/or your knowledge to explain the term more fully.
- Try to make sure that you provide at least one example in support of your answer.
- Remember, all of the marks on this question are awarded for AO1 (knowledge and understanding), so there is no need to give detailed analysis or evaluation in your answer.

The 10-mark part (b) questions

Part (b) questions instruct you to use both the extract and your own knowledge to examine briefly a particular issue or argument. Remember that 'knowledge' can include an awareness of relevant theories, concepts and political models, as well as factual examples.

How to write an A-grade answer
- Make sure that you define any relevant terms early in your answer.
- Remember, it is far better to identify three or four main points and tackle them well than to deal with six or seven points in a superficial fashion.
- Provide a clear focus on the precise terms of the question set, right from the start, perhaps by making explicit reference to words or phrases in the question itself.
- Make sure that you remember and make reference to any debates or controversies surrounding the topic under discussion.

- Do not forget that on these questions the marks for AO2 (analysis and evaluation) are equal to those for AO1 (knowledge and understanding).

The 25-mark part (c) questions

Part (c) questions are, in effect, mini-essays. The question will normally offer a short quotation (often a sentence outlining a particular point of view) followed by any one of a number of command words or instructions, e.g. 'discuss', 'assess the accuracy of this view', 'to what extent would you agree with this view?'.

How to write an A-grade answer

- As with the part (b) questions, it is important that you define any key terms early on and focus on the precise terms of the question posed from the outset. Quoting phrases or key words from the title periodically throughout your answer can be a good way of demonstrating an explicit focus.
- Make sure that you impose a clear analytical structure on your answer from the outset. Part (c) mini-essays are likely to be anywhere between one-and-a-half and two-and-a-half sides long. Adopt a structure that addresses around four factors, with one developed paragraph per factor. At the end of each paragraph ask yourself whether you have related it back to the question. If not, add a linking phrase or sentence to the end of the section.
- Try to provide some balance in your answer, i.e. avoid presenting an answer that is totally one-sided. Try to be objective, as opposed to subjective, even if you feel strongly about the issues under debate.
- Do all that you can to integrate political theory alongside supporting examples. Favouring one at the expense of the other will make it far harder for you to reach the higher levels on the mark scheme.
- Remember that on these longer questions, 6 of the 25 marks available are awarded for communication. This is not just about demonstrating sound spelling, punctuation and grammar; you also need to make use of subject-specific vocabulary.

Content
Guidance

This section of the guide aims to address the key areas of content, the central issues and the main arguments pertinent to each of the four AQA Unit 2 sections: The British constitution; Parliament; The core executive; and Multi-level governance.

While it is clearly not possible to answer every conceivable question here, this Content Guidance provides thorough yet concise coverage of all the core topics. The material is best used as the basis for further study.

The British constitution
Nature and sources
What is a constitution?

A constitution is a body of rules that defines the manner in which a state or society is organised. It sets out the way in which **sovereign power** is distributed between the government and the people, and between the government's constituent parts. However, no constitution can spell out exactly what should happen in every eventuality; it simply provides a framework upon which more complex rules, structures and processes can be built.

Codified and uncodified constitutions

There are two types of constitution. Those which take the form of a full and authoritative set of rules written down in a single document are said to be **codified**. Those which draw on a number of different sources — some written and some unwritten — are said to be **uncodified**.

The UK constitution falls into the latter category. Although it was once common to refer to the UK constitution as unwritten, the term 'uncodified' is more accurate because a significant proportion of what is considered to be constitutionally significant is in fact written in some form or another.

Codified and uncodified constitutions

Type	Nature	Format	Example
Codified	Revolutionary	A single authoritative document	USA
Uncodified	Evolutionary	A less tangible constitution, drawing upon a range of written and unwritten sources	UK

The main sources of the British constitution

The UK constitution is said to draw on five main sources.

(1) Statute law

Constitutional statute law consists of those Acts of Parliament that play a key role in defining the relationship between the government and the people or between different elements of government, e.g. the Human Rights Act (1998) or the Parliament Acts (1911 and 1949). Statute law is the supreme source of the UK constitution. Under the doctrine of **parliamentary sovereignty**, the passing of a new statute can make or unmake any existing law and overturn any other constitutional practice.

(2) Common law

Common law (often referred to as case law or 'judge-made law') refers to established customs and legal precedent developed through the actions of judges. Most of the traditional civil liberties available to UK citizens, including freedom of speech, were originally established in common law. The **royal prerogative** (including the power to declare war and agree treaties) is also rooted in common law.

(3) Conventions

Conventions are traditions or customs that have evolved over time and have become accepted rules of behaviour. Conventions have no real legal standing. As a result, they can easily be overturned with the passing of a parliamentary statute. As conventions merely reflect accepted practice, they can also fall into disuse as practices change. The doctrine of **cabinet collective responsibility** is rooted in convention.

(4) EU laws and treaties

Under the European Communities Act (1972), the UK incorporated the Treaty of Rome (1957) into UK law. This gave European laws and treaties precedence over our own national laws, although Parliament obviously reserves the right to repeal the 1972 Act and subsequent treaties, and thereby withdraw from the EU.

(5) Works of authority

Works of authority are scholarly texts which serve to codify practices not outlined on paper elsewhere. Although these works have only a persuasive authority, the fact that many of them have been used as constitutional references for well over 100 years affords them a certain status. Key texts include Walter Bagehot's *The English Constitution* (1867), Erskine May's *Parliamentary Practice* (first published in 1844) and A. V. Dicey's *An Introduction to the Study of the Law of the Constitution* (1885).

The status of constitutional sources

Though the UK constitution draws on a range of different sources, they do not have equal status or authority in establishing the overall constitutional settlement. Historically, statute law was said to be the supreme source of the UK constitution. In recent years, however, an expansion in the range and depth of EU laws and regulations has seen the primacy of statute law questioned.

Achieving constitutional change

Codified constitutions are usually said to be **entrenched**. This is generally because the process of formally amending the codified document is made difficult, often by requiring those seeking change to secure larger majorities (or 'super majorities') than would be needed to pass a regular statute. Many countries also require the **ratification** of constitutional proposals. In the USA, for example, amendments to the Constitution are formally proposed by two thirds of each chamber of the legislature (House and Senate) before being ratified by three quarters of the 50 US states (i.e. 38). In many European states, in contrast, constitutional amendments are confirmed by the means of a public vote or **referendum**.

Though the challenge of amending codifed constitutions has often led commentators to describe them as rigid, such documents can in fact be remarkably flexible. This flexibility is provided, in part, by the judiciary, who use their interpretative power to rework ageing documents and apply them to each new age. Judgements that have significant constitutional implications are therefore often referred to as **interpretative amendments**.

Changing the UK constitution

The fact that the UK constitution is uncodified makes the process of securing even far-reaching constitutional changes somewhat easier than it is on the other side of the Atlantic. Whereas in the USA, for example, the constitutional right to bear arms entrenched in the Second Amendment has obstructed those seeking to enforce US-wide restrictions on the possession of firearms, the UK Parliament was able to impose an outright ban on handguns by means of a simple Act of Parliament, passed in the wake of the murder of 16 schoolchildren and their teacher in Dunblane in 1996.

In the same way that relatively small changes such as the ban on handguns have been brought about by passing regular statute, most major constitutional changes have been secured by similar means. Although in recent years it has become more common for such statutory changes to be confirmed and legitimised by a public referendum (e.g. as with the establishment of a Scottish Parliament in 1998), this is not always the case (e.g. as happened with Lords reform) and is certainly not a legal requirement — although it is in many EU states.

The uncodified nature of the UK constitution means that significant changes can also result from the rulings of judges (i.e. through common law) or simply as a result of changing practices (i.e. evolving conventions). In consequence, whereas codified constitutions are often said to shape political practice, the reverse can also be true in the UK.

Recent constitutional reform

Labour's return to office in 1997, following 18 years in opposition, brought the prospect of a wide-ranging programme of constitutional reform.

The party's 1997 general election manifesto promised a number of significant measures, not least the possibility of House of Lords reform and a change to the first-past-the-post (simple plurality) system under which UK general elections are held. The sheer scale of Labour's victory in 1997 — the party was returned with a 179-seat Commons majority — gave it a massive popular mandate to carry such proposals into law.

Changes during New Labour's first decade in office

For many on the liberal left, Labour's return to office in 1997 appeared to offer the prospect of an entirely new constitutional settlement, perhaps comprising:

- a codified constitution
- a UK bill of rights
- an elected upper chamber
- a more proportional system for use in elections to the Westminster Parliament
- state funding of political parties
- reform of the monarchy

Set against such high expectations, the reforms introduced by the party during its first decade in office were always likely to be judged something of a disappointment — not least because there were far too many halfway houses and unfinished projects.

That said, one should not underestimate the significant changes that were made, all of which are dealt with more fully either in later sections of this guide or in the companion guide to AQA AS Unit 1 (GOVP1).

Parliament

Lords reform saw all but 92 hereditary peers lose their right to sit and vote in the chamber (the House of Lords Act, 1999). A second stage of Lords reform stalled in 2003 when Parliament rejected all eight models for a reformed chamber. Attempts to revive the reform process in 2007 again ran aground when the Commons voted for an entirely elected second chamber and the Lords gave its support to an entirely appointed model. At the end of New Labour's first decade in power, Lords reform was still essentially where is was following the House of Lords Act (1999).

Elections and referendums

The Jenkins Commission's suggestion that AV+ should be adopted for general elections was not acted upon, though hybrid systems were instituted in other UK elections, e.g. AMS (FPTP-top up) in elections to the Scottish Parliament and Welsh Assembly. Labour made extensive use of referendums. It also established an independent **Electoral Commission** under the Political Parties, Elections and Referendums Act (PPERA, 2000). This body was charged with the task of monitoring elections, regulating party funding and expenditure, and organising referendums.

Rights

The Human Rights Act (HRA, 1998) incorporated most of the provisions of the European Convention on Human Rights into UK law. This meant that citizens could seek redress in UK courts without having to go to the European Court of Human Rights in Strasbourg. The Freedom of Information Act (FOIA, 2000) gave citizens the right to request information held by public bodies.

Devolution

A Scottish Parliament and a Welsh Assembly were established. London was given an elected mayor, a strategic authority (the Greater London Authority) and a 25-member elected assembly (the Greater London Assembly). The Northern Ireland Act (1998) established a Northern Ireland Assembly and power-sharing executive.

Influencing and limiting government powers

The uncodified and unentrenched nature of the UK constitution clearly has a bearing on whether or not it can truly limit the powers of government. In the absence of a codified constitutional document, statute law remains the highest constitutional source in the UK. In consequence, any government with a working majority in the House of Commons has the legal authority and power to reshape the constitution as it sees fit, simply by passing regular statute through Parliament.

The extent to which governments are constrained by the constitutional arrangements present in the UK will be discussed in more detail later in this guide, when we consider the power of the judiciary and the scope and extent of parliamentary power. It is, however, helpful at this stage to outline briefly the main principles of the UK constitution, which will provide the necessary context for the discussion that follows.

Principles of the UK constitution

(1) Parliamentary sovereignty
Rooted in common law, the doctrine of parliamentary sovereignty is based upon three interlocking principles:
- Parliament can make or unmake any UK law.
- Only Parliament can make UK law.
- No Parliament can bind its successors.

(2) Parliamentary government under a constitutional monarch
A parliamentary government is one in which the government operates on the basis of a mandate granted periodically through free and fair elections. In Britain, our **bicameral** Parliament operates alongside a constitutional monarch. The monarchy remains part of Parliament — technically at least ('the Queen in Parliament') — but unlike its medieval counterpart, the modern monarchy is strictly controlled in what it can do, both by statute and through convention. As a result, though the monarchy legally retains wide-ranging powers, it has long since become what Walter Bagehot referred to as a 'dignified' part of the constitution; that is to say, it has become largely symbolic or ceremonial, with its formal powers exercised by others.

(3) The rule of law
According to A. V. Dicey (1885), the rule of law has three main strands:
- First, that no one can be punished without trial.
- Second, that no one is above the law and all are subject to the same justice.
- Third, that the general principles of the constitution (e.g. personal freedoms) result from the decisions of judges (i.e. case law or common law) rather than from parliamentary statute or executive order.

(4) The unitary state

Britain is said to be a **unitary state** as opposed to a **federal** one. This means that all ultimate power in the UK is held by the central government at Westminster. Any power that local government or regional government appears to have is merely delegated or 'devolved' to it and can, in theory at least, be withdrawn at any time.

Are the constitutional principles under threat?

It is said that the passage of the European Communities Act (1972) undermined parliamentary sovereignty. This is because the Act incorporated the Treaty of Rome (1957) into UK law, thereby giving European law precedence over UK statute where the two are in conflict. Eurosceptics fear that the extension of qualified majority voting in the council of ministers further reduces the UK Parliament's ability to prevent Europe-wide policies being imposed upon UK citizens. While a UK withdrawal from the EU could be secured with the passage of a regular statute, such a move would be difficult to execute in practice.

We will return to the theme of EU law later in this guide, and consider as well the way in which developments since 1972 — not least the Maastricht Treaty (1992), the proposed EU Constitution (2004) and the Lisbon Treaty (2007) that replaced it — have added to the debate over national sovereignty.

Though Britain still has parliamentary government under a constitutional monarch, the ongoing process of parliamentary reform, the increased use of referendums since 1997, the rise of executive dominance, and increasingly savage media criticism of the royal family, have all signalled change in this area.

The specific limitations placed upon the rights of those accused or even suspected under the various pieces of anti-terrorist legislation is just one of the longstanding exceptions to the rule of law.

Though the UK remains, in theory, a unitary state, considerable power has been devolved to bodies such as the Scottish Parliament in such a way that it would be difficult to withdraw.

The judiciary and its relationship to other government 'powers'

The organisation of the UK judiciary

In its simplest sense, the term **'judiciary'** is a collective noun referring to all UK judges, from lay magistrates right the way up to the Law Lords. In a wider sense, it can be taken to mean all those who are directly involved in the administration and application of justice.

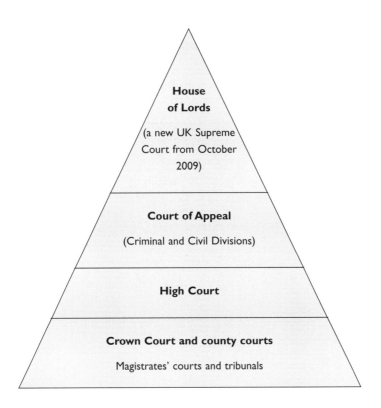

House
of Lords

(a new UK Supreme
Court from October
2009)

Court of Appeal

(Criminal and Civil Divisions)

High Court

Crown Court and county courts

Magistrates' courts and tribunals

- Judges at all levels are involved in ensuring that justice is done and the law is properly applied.
- At the lower levels of the judiciary, the main role of judges is to preside over trials, give guidance to the jury and impose sentences.
- At the High Court level, judges hear more serious cases and can also hear cases on appeal.
- At the Court of Appeal level and above, judges are concerned with clarifying the meaning of the law, rather than just applying it. These courts can set precedent.
- Cases heard in the Court of Appeal normally result from confusion in the lower courts regarding the meaning of a law. The Court of Appeal also deals with major cases arising from the Human Rights Act (HRA, 1998).
- The Law Lords hear cases on appeal from the Appeals Court. In recent years such disputes have increasingly been brought under the HRA (1998) or under EU law. Those serving as Law Lords in October 2009 are set to become the first members of the new UK Supreme Court, located in Middlesex Guildhall.

It is the higher levels of the judiciary (i.e. the top two tiers of the pyramid) that are of most concern to politics students. This is because these higher tiers have the power to set legal precedent, thereby establishing common law; they clarify the meaning of the law as opposed to simply applying the letter of the law.

What is civil law?

Civil law is concerned with interrelationships between different individuals and groups. Civil cases generally involve matters such as wills or contracts. Most successful cases result in compensation awards.

(1) County courts

These deal with small-scale civil cases, including disputes over small contracts, wills, and many divorce cases. They are presided over by circuit or district judges.

(2) High Court

This hears more complex cases or those referred to it by county courts. The High Court has three divisions: the Queen's Bench Division, the Family Division and the Chancery Division. Its hearings are presided over by one or more High Court judge.

(3) Court of Appeal

The Civil Division of the Court of Appeal hears civil cases on appeal from lower courts.

What is criminal law?

Criminal law deals with crimes by an individual or group against the state, e.g. violent behaviour, serious fraud or burglary. Such cases are normally brought by the state and can lead to fines and imprisonment.

(1) Magistrates' courts

These hear most minor criminal cases (98% of the total). Magistrates also have the task of identifying cases that are indictable.

(2) Crown courts

These deal with more serious criminal cases and appeals from magistrates' courts.

(3) Court of Appeal

The Criminal Division of the Court of Appeal hears criminal cases on appeal from lower courts.

The Appellate Committee of the House of Lords

The House of Lords — or, more accurately, the Appellate Committee of the House of Lords — has traditionally been positioned at the apex of both the civil and criminal court hierarchies as the ultimate court of appeal within the UK judicial system. Indeed, only the European Court of Justice — and only then in matters concerning EU law — has had the power to overrule the House of Lords.

The twelve Lords of Appeal in Ordinary (the **'Law Lords'**), who sit on the Appellate Committee of the House of Lords, have traditionally performed a similar role to US Supreme Court Justices. They hear appeals referred to them by the Court of Appeal (both Criminal and Civil Divisions) and thereby clarify the meaning of contentious points of law.

In most instances, a panel of 5 of the 12 Law Lords is selected to consider a case, though it is not unheard of for additional Law Lords to be drafted in where the case is particularly serious or complex. For example, in December 2004, an appellate committee of 9 Law Lords ruled (8:1) that the indefinite detention of suspects under the Anti-Terrorism, Crime and Security Act (2001) was incompatible with Articles 5 and 14 of the Human Rights Act (1998).

Though British politics textbooks have often referred to the House of Lords as the UK's 'Supreme Court', this label often leads to confusion — not least among those failing to grasp fully the difference between the legislative work of the upper chamber and the judicial work of the Appellate Committee. The fact that the UK's highest court of appeal is hidden within the legislature has further denied UK citizens the kind of iconic and independent Supreme Court enjoyed by those in the USA. Such issues have been addressed through the creation of a new UK Supreme Court under the Constitutional Reform Act (2005).

The new UK Supreme Court

At the start of the legal year in October 2009, the 12 Law Lords who comprise the House of Lords Appellate Committee will move to new accommodation in the renovated Middlesex Guildhall, opposite the Houses of Parliament. Though they will remain members of the Lords, they will at the same time become the first justices of the new UK Supreme Court.

The creation of a new UK Supreme Court was one of many measures set out in the Constitutional Reform Act (CRA) (2005). Under this Act the new UK Supreme Court will take on the four roles previously performed by the Law Lords:

- act as the final court of appeal in England, Wales and Northern Ireland
- hear appeals on issues of public importance surrounding arguable points of law
- hear appeals from civil cases in England, Wales, Northern Ireland and Scotland
- hear appeals from criminal cases in England, Wales and Northern Ireland (the High Court of Justiciary will retain jurisdiction over criminal cases in Scotland)

In addition, the Supreme Court will take on the role that the Judicial Committee of the Privy Council has performed in resolving disputes between the devolved governments of Northern Ireland, Scotland and Wales, and the UK Parliament. The Privy Council Committee will, however, retain jurisdiction over Commonwealth cases.

The creation of a new UK Supreme Court — benefiting from a new, independent appointments process and accommodated in a separate building — will go some way towards addressing criticisms traditionally levelled at the Lords, not least by providing for a greater separation of powers.

Judicial appointments

The **senior judiciary** comprises Lords of Appeal in Ordinary (Law Lords), Heads of Divisions, Lords Justices of Appeal, High Court judges and deputy High Court judges. Senior judicial appointments were traditionally made by the monarch on the advice of the prime minister and the Lord Chancellor. The Lord Chancellor customarily consulted serving senior judges through a process known as 'secret soundings'.

Though lower-level vacancies in the senior judiciary (e.g. for High Court judges) were advertised, the Lord Chancellor was under no obligation to appoint from among those who had formally applied. It was said that this system lacked transparency, compromised the proper separation of powers, and resulted in the senior judiciary being drawn almost exclusively from a narrow social circle: public school and Oxbridge educated, white, middle-aged men.

Reforming judicial appointments

In 2003 Labour announced plans to transfer the Lord Chancellor's power over senior judicial appointments to a new, independent **Judicial Appointments Commission** (JAC). It was hoped that these changes, brought into law by the Constitutional Reform Act (2005), might eventually result in a senior judiciary that was more representative of the broader population.

In spite of this stated intention, early indications based upon the work of the JAC suggest that the process of creating a judiciary that 'looks like the UK' might take some time. On 28 January 2008, the *Guardian* reported that the new JAC had approved 21 individuals to become High Court judges and that 10 of these had already been given posts. Of these 10:
- All were white, male, and former barristers.
- Of the nine educated in Britain, six went to leading independent schools belonging to the Headmasters' and Headmistresses' Conference (HMC).

In evidence to the Justice Select Committee in 2008, Justice Minister Jack Straw conceded that, of those recommended for judicial appointments at all levels by the JAC in its first year (2006–07):
- only 8% were from black or Asian backgrounds (compared to 14% in 2005–06)
- only 34% were women (compared to 41% in 2005–06)

In response, the JAC maintained that it has appointed 'on merit and merit alone [using] selection processes that are open and fair to all applicants, regardless of their gender, race or background'.

Appointments to the new UK Supreme Court

The first Justices of the Supreme Court will be the 12 Law Lords already in-post when the move into new accommodation happens in October 2009. Under the CRA (2005), the most senior of the 12 will take on the role of president of the Court, with the second most senior assuming the role of deputy president.

Though these 12 former Law Lords will remain members of the upper house, they will be barred from sitting and voting in the legislature for as long as they remain Justices of the Supreme Court. Those appointed subsequently to the Supreme Court will not be made members of the Lords.

Qualifications for office

To be considered for appointment as a Justice of the Supreme Court, candidates must have either:

(1) held high judicial office for at least two years

or:

(2) been a qualifying practitioner for a period of 15 years

Qualifying practitioners are one of the following:
- holder of a Senior Courts qualification
- advocates in Scotland or solicitors entitled to appear in the Scottish Court of Session and the High Court of Justiciary
- member of the Bar of Northern Ireland or a solicitor of the Court of Judicature of Northern Ireland

The Selection Commission

Vacancies in the Supreme Court will be filled by a Selection Commission separate from the JAC that was created to select other members of the senior judiciary. According to Schedule 8, Part 1 of the CRA (2005), this ad hoc, five-member commission will comprise:

(1) the president of the Supreme Court

(2) the deputy president of the Supreme Court

(3) one member of the Judicial Appointments Commission (JAC)

(4) one member of the Judicial Appointments Board for Scotland

(5) one member of the Northern Ireland Judicial Appointments Commission

The appointments process

Though the appointments process will still involve the minister who formally holds the title of Lord Chancellor (i.e. the Justice Minister), the minister's role is to be greatly reduced.

Under this new system:

(1) A vacancy arises.

(2) A 5-member Selection Commission is convened to consider possible nominees and make a 'selection' based on merit.

(3) The commission submits a report to the Lord Chancellor naming a nominee.

(4) The Lord Chancellor has three options:
  (a) to accept the selection by 'notifying' the prime minister
  (b) to reject the selection
  (c) to require the commission to reconsider its selection.

(5) Once 'notified' — under option (a) — the prime minister *must* recommend the approved candidate to the Queen.

(6) The individual is appointed a Justice of the Supreme Court when Her Majesty issues letters patent.

Although on paper this appears to leave the Lord Chancellor with considerable power as regards appointments to the new Court, the reality is rather more complicated, as he or she is not permitted to reject repeatedly names put forward by the commission. Precisely what the Lord Chancellor can and cannot do is addressed in more detail in Chapter 6 of the *2008 UK Government & Politics Annual Survey* by P. Fairclough, R. Kelly and E. Magee (Philip Allan Updates).

Note that in 2007 the then minister for Justice and Lord Chancellor Jack Straw indicated that he intended to use this system to appoint regular Law Lords, where vacancies arose, ahead of the formal opening of the Supreme Court in 2009.

The relationship of the judiciary to the executive and the legislature

Judicial review in the UK

Whereas the US Supreme Court can void Acts of Congress, UK courts cannot declare parliamentary statutes unconstitutional. This is because statute law is the supreme source of constitutional law in the UK.

What UK courts can do is review the actions of government officials in order to decide whether or not they have acted unlawfully, that is **ultra vires** (beyond the authority given to them under the law).

EU membership and judicial power

Under the European Communities Act (1972), the UK incorporated the Treaty of Rome into UK Law. The effect of this was to give European laws precedence over conflicting UK statutes, whether past or present. Before 1990, this meant that the European Court of Justice could challenge UK statutes. Following the *Factortame* case (1990), UK Courts have also been able to suspend UK statutes that appear to be in violation of EU law.

The *Factortame* case (1990)

The case grew out of a complaint by Spanish fishermen that the Merchant Shipping Act (1988) violated the Single European Act (1986) in requiring vessels using UK fishing quotas to re-register and meet certain nationality requirements.

The High Court referred the case to the European Court of Justice (ECJ) and told the Transport Secretary not to apply key sections of the Act until a final ruling.

The House of Lords overturned this instruction, arguing that no UK court had the power to suspend statute — at least until the ECJ could make a final determination.

In 1990, the ECJ ruled that UK courts do have the power to suspend Acts of Parliament that appear to break EU law.

The Human Rights Act and judicial power

Under the Human Rights Act (HRA) (1998), UK courts now have the right to issue a **declaration of incompatibility** where a parliamentary statute appears to violate the rights set out in the HRA. Parliament is not, however, obliged to amend the offending statute.

The impact of the Human Rights Act and the European Court of Human Rights upon the British political system

The European Convention on Human Rights (ECHR)

The ECHR was established by the Council of Europe in 1950. The Council of Europe is an intergovernmental body that is totally separate from the European Union and should *not* be confused with the EU's Council of Ministers or the European Council.

Alleged violations of the ECHR are investigated by the **European Commission on Human Rights** and tried in the **European Court of Human Rights**, based in Strasbourg. Again, these bodies are *not* to be confused with the EU's European Commission and European Court of Justice. The latter, based in Luxembourg, is the highest court of the EU, ensuring the uniform interpretation and application of EU law and adjudicating disputes between member states.

The Human Rights Act (1998)

The HRA was passed in 1998 and came into force in October 2000. It incorporated most of the articles of the ECHR into UK law, thereby allowing citizens to pursue cases under the ECHR through UK courts, as opposed to having to go directly to the European Court of Human Rights.

As the HRA is based upon the Council of Europe's ECHR, rather than on EU law, it is *not* superior to parliamentary statute, as EU laws are under the Treaty of Rome. Despite this, the HRA (like the ECHR) has a **persuasive authority** that has enhanced the protection of individual rights in the UK.

The HRA in action

The HRA does not have the same legal status as EU law or the US Bill of Rights, the latter being both entrenched and superior to regular statute. But although the courts cannot void parliamentary statute under the HRA, they can make a declaration of incompatibility and invite Parliament to reconsider the offending statute. Where statute is silent, or unclear, the courts can make even greater use of the HRA.

Crucially, under Article 15 of the ECHR, national governments are permitted to derogate some of the convention's articles in times of national crisis. Part 4 of the UK's Anti-Terrorism, Crime and Security Act (2001), for example, was only passed after the government opted to derogate Article 5 of the HRA on the grounds that there was a 'public emergency threatening the life of the nation'. This phrase, which met the requirements set out in Article 15, meant that the 2001 Act could authorise the indefinite detention without trial of foreign nationals whom the home secretary judged were involved in terrorism.

Though things have clearly moved on in this respect since 2001 (see the box on p. 32), it remains the case that the HRA does not give the courts the necessary power to stop or overturn government action.

The courts, the HRA and the detention of terrorist suspects

- The passage of the UK's Anti-Terrorism, Crime and Security Act (2001), Part 4, allowed the indefinite detention, without trial, of foreign nationals whom the home secretary judged were involved in terrorism.
- This measure could only be passed because the government was able to derogate Article 5 of the Human Rights Act on the grounds that there was a 'public emergency threatening the life of the nation', which met the requirements set out in Article 15.
- In December 2004, an Appellate Committee of 9 Law Lords ruled (8:1) that the indefinite detention of suspects under the Anti-Terrorism, Crime and Security Act (2001) was incompatible with Articles 5 and 14 of the HRA.
- In June and August 2006 the High Court found that the control orders brought in as part of the 2005 Prevention of Terrorism Act also violated Article 5, as they were tantamount to imprisonment without trial — though the government chose not to remove such control orders.

Source: P. Fairclough in P. Fairclough, R. Kelly and E. Magee, *2007 UK Government & Politics Annual Survey* (Philip Allan Updates)

The HRA has also been used in a number of non-terrorist-related cases, e.g. in the granting of lifelong anonymity to the killers of the toddler Jamie Bulger.

The articles in question of the HRA	Newspapers had argued that **Article 10** of the HRA gave them the right to publish details relating to the whereabouts and new identities of the two young men who had killed the toddler Jamie Bulger when they were aged 10. The court disagreed. Granting a lifetime ban on the publication of such information, the court argued that identifying the two men might threaten their lives (violating **Article 2**) and possibly subject them to inhuman and degrading treatment (violating **Article 3**). It was also argued that such a ban might help protect their right to a private and family life (under **Article 8**).
Article 2: right to life **Article 3:** prohibition of torture **Article 8:** respect for private and family life **Article 10:** freedom of expression	

Judicial independence and neutrality

Judicial independence is the principle that those in the judiciary should be **free from political control**. Such independence allows judges to 'do the right thing' and apply justice properly, without fear of the consequences.

Judicial neutrality is where judges operate **impartially** (i.e. without personal bias) when administering justice. This is necessary as part of the rule of law, by which:

- everyone is equal under the law
- no one is above the law
- everyone is entitled to a free and fair trial

The absence of judicial independence threatens judicial neutrality, because if judges are being controlled they are not able to be impartial. However, judicial independence does not guarantee judicial neutrality — judges may still allow their personal views to influence their administering of justice.

How is the independence of the judiciary maintained?
In theory, judicial independence results from a number of different factors:

- Judges' **security of tenure**: it is extraordinarily hard for judges at High Court level and above (i.e. the senior judiciary) to be removed. Indeed, this can only take place as a result of impeachment proceedings requiring a vote in both houses of Parliament. Those in more junior ranks of the judiciary can be removed by the Lord Chancellor and the Lord Chief Justice. On 17 May 2008 the _Guardian_ reported the results of a Freedom of Information Act (2000) request, confirming that two junior judges had been dismissed for misconduct in 2005.
- **Guaranteed salaries**: judges' salaries are free from political manipulation, being drawn from the Consolidated Fund.
- **Contempt of court**: under _sub judice_ rules it is an offence for ministers and others to speak out publicly during the course of legal proceedings.
- An increasingly **independent appointments system** under the JAC (see p. 28).
- The **training and experience** of senior judges — the pride they take in their role and in their personal legal reputation.

Parliament

Role in the UK's political system

Composition: the Commons

At the time of the 2005 general election, the Commons comprised 646 MPs, each MP representing one single-member constituency. This total was 13 seats fewer than had been contested at the previous general election in 2001 (i.e. 659).

The reduction, achieved entirely through redrawing Scottish electoral districts, was intended as a partial remedy for the issue of double representation north of the border. This problem, commonly referred to as the **West Lothian Question**, resulted from the establishment of a Scottish Parliament with primary legislative powers (see p. 63).

Composition of the House of Commons by party in 2005 and 2008

Party	2005 general election	22 April 2008
Labour	355	351
Conservative	198	192
Liberal Democrat	62	63
Democratic Unionist	9	9
Scottish National Party	6	6
Sinn Fein	5	5
Plaid Cymru	3	3
Social Democratic and Labour Party	3	3
Independent	2	3
Ulster Unionist	1	1
Respect	1	1
UK Independence	0	1
Speaker (+ deputies)	1	1 (+3)
Vacant	0	1
Working majority	**64**	**66**

Source: House of Commons website, accessed 3 May 2008

Socioeconomic background of MPs

(i) Age: the youngest MP elected in 2005 was Jo Swinson (25), a LibDem in East Dunbartonshire. In 2005 the average age of those returned as MPs was 50.6.

(ii) Gender: in 1987 only 6% of MPs (41) were women. In 2005 the figure was 19% (125), up from 18% (119) in 2004.

(iii) Ethnicity and religion: the Commons remains a disproportionately white and Christian chamber. In 2005, for example, only five black MPs (four Labour and the first ever black Conservative MP) were returned. The new Commons contained only four Muslims.

Does the composition of the Commons need to reflect the broader population?

The resemblance theory of representation holds that those in the legislature should be typical of the communities that they serve. Thus, it is argued, they can reflect more fully their communities' collective values and beliefs.

There are any number of reasons why the young, women, ethnic minorities and those from non-Christian faiths might be so underrepresented in the Commons — and not all of these are to do with ageism, sexism or racism. A bigger question is whether or not this failure to elect a Commons that reflects the composition of the broader population is really a problem.

Yes, resemblance is important
- A more representative Commons will better understand the issues facing some communities.
- Some ethnic minorities may have more faith in the legislature.

No, resemblance is not important
- Some constituents will always be represented by people who are unlike them.
- A good MP will represent all constituents to the best of their ability, irrespective of ethnicity, religion or gender.

Composition: the Lords

Immediately prior to Lords reform in 1999, the Conservatives had 471 peers to Labour's 179. This **inbuilt Tory majority**, as it was commonly referred to, consisted largely of Conservative hereditary peers. Critics argued that many of these peers ('backwoodsmen') attended only when they were needed to block radical legislation. The removal of the hereditary peers as a result of the House of Lords Act (1999), and the subsequent appointment of a large number of Labour life peers, has changed the chamber significantly (see the table below). That said, one should remember that factors such as the Lords' security of tenure mean that party ties are, in any case, relatively weak.

Composition of the House of Lords by party (1 May 2008)

Party	Number
Conservative	202
Labour	217
Liberal Democrat	78
Crossbench	196
UK Independence	2
Conservative Independent	1
Independent Labour	1
Non-affiliated	9
Total	**706**

Note: excluding 13 peers on leave of absence and 26 bishops

Appointment

The process by which life peers are appointed dates from the **1958 Life Peerages Act**. Though it is technically the monarch who confers life peerages, the prime minister has a virtually free rein. Though he/she is bound by convention to invite nominations from opposition parties and the nominees are scrutinised by the House of Lords Appointments Commission, neither check presents an insurmountable obstacle.

The House of Lords by type (1 May 2008)

Type	Men	Women	Total
Life peers under the Life Peerages Act (1958)	461	144	605
Peers under the House of Lords Act (1999)	89	2	91
Life peers under the Appellate Jurisdiction Act (1876)	22	1	23
Archbishops and bishops	26	0	26
Total	**598**	**147**	**745**

Note: excluding one seat under the House of Lords Act (1999), which was vacant

Labour and the appointment of life peers (1997–2005)
The process by which life peers are appointed is criticised by many as being no better a method for selecting legislators than the hereditary principle it was designed to replace. The rapid increase in the number of Labour peers since 1997 led to accusations of **cronyism** ('Tony's cronies') or even that peerages were being sold in return for political donations or loans — though the latter was ultimately unproven. The introduction of so-called 'peoples' peers' was supposed to address the problem of cronyism, but Blair's elevation of special advisor Andrew Adonis to the Lords in 2005, and straight into the government as education minister, reignited the debate.

Using the power to appoint peers
The power to appoint life peers can be used for the following:
- as a means of **bringing people into the cabinet** without waiting for a Commons by-election (e.g. Gus MacDonald, Andrew Adonis)
- as a device for **getting rid of potentially troublesome Commons backbenchers** (e.g. the elevation to the Lords of former leaders such as Margaret Thatcher)
- as a **reward for political service** (e.g. Blair's private pollster Philip Gould, in 2004)

The main roles and functions of Parliament

Parliament performs three main roles or functions within the UK system:
(1) **Representation**: Commons MPs are elected to serve a geographical constituency and those who live there. MPs should represent the concerns of their constituents within Parliament.
(2) **Legislation:** Parliament's primary function as a legislature is to legislate. Though most of a government's legislative programme will be uncontroversial, it must still

pass through both chambers — unless the Parliament Act is invoked — before it can become law.

(3) Scrutiny: Parliament plays an important role in scrutinising the government through parliamentary committees and other procedures (e.g. Prime Minister's Questions).

It also has two other roles:

(4) Legitimisation: in the UK the government is not elected directly. This means that its legitimacy rests upon the confidence of the Commons, the withdrawal of which (i.e. through a vote of no confidence) causes the government to fall (e.g. the end of James Callaghan's Labour Government in 1979).

(5) Political recruitment: Parliament provides the recruiting pool from which all members of the government are drawn. Most ministers will have served an apprenticeship in the Commons before taking high office, though some may be brought into the Lords as a means of bringing them into Parliament (e.g. Andrew Adonis in 2005).

The legislative process

Different types of bill

Public bills affect the entire population:

(1) Government bills: these often seek to fulfil manifesto commitments and are more likely to succeed because the government controls the parliamentary timetable. Ministers pilot these bills through Parliament.

(2) Private Member's Bills: introduced by any MP on any issue, these bills rarely succeed without government support (due to time pressures). They can offer a useful way of legislating on issues of conscience, e.g. the Abortion Act (1967).

Private bills affect particular areas of policy or a specified organisation, as opposed to the population as a whole. Some private bills (called 'personal bills') deal only with regulations affecting one or two people (e.g. granting a dispensation from existing law).

Normal passage of legislation

(1) First reading in the Commons (formal introduction; date for second reading set).

(2) Second reading (minister outlines principles of bill; debate follows).

(3) Standing committee (committee scrutinises and, if necessary, amends the bill before reporting to the Commons).

(4) Third reading (no major amendments at this stage; bill passed or rejected).

(5) House of Lords (same process as in the Commons, though the committee stage is often taken on the floor of House). Amendments back to the Commons. Then back to the Lords, who approve or reject the bill (possible use of Parliament Act at this stage).

(6) Royal assent.

Short-cutting the legislative process

Though it often takes a considerable amount of time to move a proposal from the Green Paper stage to the statute books, the government of the day is able to speed up the process if it is prepared to use the powers available by virtue of its Commons majority. These are:

- **Whip** the standing committee to ensure speedy passage.
- Formally **guillotine** committee action.
- **Limit time** for Commons debate.
- Make **concessions** to backbenchers and/or the Lords.
- Threaten the use of and/or use the **Parliament Act**.

That said, both the Commons and the Lords are still able to flex their muscles on controversial legislation (see below).

Prevention of Terrorism Bill (2005)

Over 28½ hours on 10–11 March 2005, the longest 'day' in Parliament since Labour came to power in 1997, the Prevention of Terrorism Bill ping-ponged between the Commons and the Lords.

The Commons saw Labour rebellions on 11 of the 12 separate votes. Seven Labour MPs — Jeremy Corbyn, Kate Hoey, Kelvin Hopkins, Glenda Jackson, Bob Marshall-Andrews, Brian Sedgemore and Clare Short — opposed the government on all 11 divisions.

It was the Lords, however, which forced what was hailed as a 'sunset clause' in all but name. Under this amendment, Parliament will have the opportunity to review or repeal the measure at a later date.

Source: adapted from P. Cowley and M. Stuart (www.revolts.co.uk)

Relative powers of the House of Commons and the House of Lords

The two chambers in the UK legislature do not have co-equal legislative power. Though the Lords was once the pre-eminent chamber, its unelected status in a time of widening Commons franchise led to a number of developments that have limited the Lords' power.

The Parliament Acts of 1911 and 1949

The **1911 Parliament Act** resulted from the Lords' attempt to block the government's budget in 1909. The Act replaced the Lords' right to veto legislation with the power to delay bills for two years. At the same time the Lords was effectively prevented from vetoing, amending or delaying money bills. This underpinned the

Commons' financial privilege; its right to deal with money bills first. The **Parliament Act of 1949** reduced the power of delay to one parliamentary session.

Though the Parliament Acts give the Commons ultimate power over the Lords, this power was only used on four occasions between 1949 and 2005: over the War Crimes Act (1991), the European Parliamentary Elections Act (1999), the Sexual Offences (Amendment) Act (2000) and the Hunting Act (2004).

The Salisbury Doctrine

Dating from 1945, the Salisbury Doctrine established the convention that the Lords — as an unelected chamber — should not oppose government bills at second reading where the government had established a clear electoral mandate to act by including a measure in its manifesto.

Is the Lords really that weak?

Though the Parliament Acts and the Salisbury Doctrine provide real checks on the power of the Lords, its experience, its security of tenure and the relatively weak party ties in the Chamber make it a serious obstacle to the government. The Lords proved particularly effective in holding Conservative governments to account between 1979 and 1997 and provided a similarly formidable barrier to New Labour's legislative programme after 1997. In the modern era, where large Commons majorities have become the norm, many have come to regard the Lords as the real opposition within Parliament.

Government defeats in the Lords to 1 May 2008

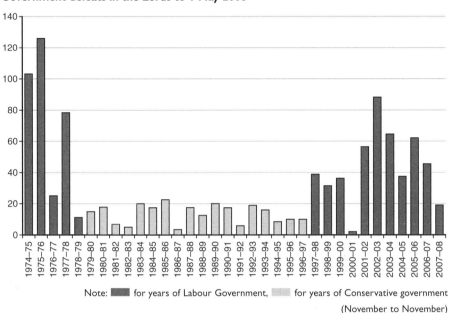

Note: ▮ for years of Labour Government, ▯ for years of Conservative government

(November to November)

Parliamentary reform since 1997

The first stage of Lords reform

Prior to the passage of the **House of Lords Act (1999)**, the upper chamber included 759 hereditary peers among its 1,330 members. It was the apparent inequity of the hereditary principle — and the fact that the unreformed upper house contained 471 Conservative peers to Labour's 179 — which had prompted Labour's 1997 manifesto commitment to both remove the rights of hereditary peers to sit and vote in the House of Lords and to move towards a more democratic and more representative second chamber. The House of Lords Act (1999) sought to deliver on the first of these promises, though under the Weatherill Amendment, 92 hereditaries were allowed to stay on in a transitional House prior to further reform.

The second stage of Lords reform

Following the report of the Wakeham Commission (2000), Labour's **2001 White Paper** proposed a second chamber consisting of 600 members, 20% of whom would be directly elected, the remainder being appointed under the auspices — though not control — of an Independent Appointments Commission. Amid accusations of cronyism, opposition parties demanded an 80%-elected chamber. The Commons was ultimately presented with eight models, ranging from a fully elected chamber to its total abolition. On 4 February 2003 it rejected all eight proposals.

In its 2005 general election manifesto, Labour promised that a 'predominantly elected' second chamber would replace the Lords. This pledge eventually found form in the **2007 White Paper** on Lords reform. The highlights of the paper were:

- The House of Commons to **retain its primacy** over legislation.
- An upper chamber split **50:50** between elected and appointed members, serving a single fixed term, far longer than that enjoyed by those in the Commons (perhaps 12 years).
- **Elections** to be held under a partially open regional list system and staggered in three cohorts.
- Appointments to be made by a new independent **Statutory Appointments Commission**, with 20% of those chosen being non-political appointees.
- A chamber where **no single party** would be allowed to enjoy an **overall majority**.

Although there appeared to be a degree of cross-party agreement ahead of the free votes offered in the Commons and the Lords on these proposals, the votes effectively left Lords reform deadlocked once more (see the table below):

- The Commons voted by a majority of 113 in favour of an entirely elected second chamber, with some MPs clearly backing a fully elected chamber as a wrecking tactic designed to antagonise the Lords.
- The Lords rejected all of the proposed models apart from the one under which the second chamber would remain entirely appointed.

	Commons (7 March 2007)			Lords (14 March 2007)		
	For	Against	Majority	For	Against	Majority
Abolition	163	416	−253	No vote taken		
All appointed	196	375	−179	361	121	240
50% elected	155	418	−263	46	409	−363
60% elected	178	392	−214	45	392	−347
80% elected	305	267	+38	114	336	−222
All elected	337	224	+113	122	326	−204

Why has it proven so hard to complete the second stage of Lords reform?
Though Labour's 1997 manifesto committed the party to removing the rights of hereditary peers as a first step — regardless of any further changes — critics argue that it was a mistake to embark on reform of the second chamber without some clear idea of where it was leading. Though the voting rights of the remaining hereditary peers may not remain forever, further reform is problematic for two main reasons:

- there is no real consensus about the best way forward
- there is a general sense that the transitional chamber has performed its functions well

Parliamentary sovereignty in theory and practice

For A. V. Dicey, the doctrine of parliamentary sovereignty is one of the 'twin pillars' of the English constitution and the rule of law. As we saw earlier in this guide, parliamentary sovereignty is rooted in common law and based on three interlocking principles:

- Parliament can make or unmake any UK law.
- Only Parliament can make UK law.
- No Parliament can bind its successors.

In recent years, however, some commentators have questioned the extent to which this doctrine is still a reality. The superiority of EU law over UK statute, New Labour's devolution programme and the increased use of referendums in the UK since the 1970s are all said to have undermined Parliament's position at the apex of the UK system of government. Though in theory Parliament still has the power necessary to reverse all of these changes — and therefore retains legal sovereignty — in practice it is unlikely to do so.

We will return to this issue again when we consider the nature of multi-level governance (see pp. 61–72).

Parliament and government relationships

The scrutiny of legislation and holding government to account

Commons committees

Committees in the House of Commons are often said to pale in comparison to their counterparts in the US House of Representatives. Congressional committees have far better financial resources, a larger body of dedicated support staff and a number of additional powers, most notably the legal power of subpoena — the right to demand that witnesses are brought forward and evidence is made available. Despite such unfavourable comparisons, Commons committees still play an important role in scrutinising legislation and holding the government to account.

Standing committees

Commons standing committees are ad hoc rather than permanent. They are formed to consider specific pieces of legislation and disband when their work is complete. Standing committees normally consist of 15–25 members; the numbers from each party reflect the composition of the House itself, and they are appointed by the Committee of Selection (which consists of experienced MPs).

Most bills pass to a standing committee following the second reading stage in the Commons. Standing committees consider each clause of a bill in turn, though — as we saw earlier — the government can apply a guillotine to limit the time that a bill spends in committee. The whipping of committee members means that amendments are unlikely to succeed without government support.

Select committees

Select committees are not involved in the passage of legislation, but they play a vital role in holding the government to account. Departmental select committees have had the role of scrutinising the work of specific government departments since they were established in the 1970s. Both the Norton Report (2000) and the Newton Report (2001) proposed a widening and strengthening of departmental select committees. Of the non-departmental select committees, the Public Accounts Committee is one of the most high profile. It has the role of ensuring value for money in government. This committee has developed a fearsome reputation for making departments accountable for their spending.

Prime Minister's Questions (PMQs) and ministers' questions

Each Wednesday, for 30 minutes, MPs are given the opportunity to quiz the premier at Prime Minister's Questions (PMQs). This single weekly slot was introduced during New Labour's first term in office as a replacement for the twice-weekly 15-minute slots that were previously timetabled on Tuesdays and Thursdays. Although the single longer slot was supposed to offer the opportunity for more lengthy and meaningful questioning of the prime minister, PMQs are still widely seen as theatre rather than real politics. That said, they do afford backbenchers and leading opposition figures the opportunity to raise issues that concern their constituents and thereby hold the prime minister and his government to account. PMQs also provide a chance for front-benchers to make a name for themselves and put the prime minister on the spot — as did LibDem caretaker leader Vince Cable in 2007 with his observation that Gordon Brown had transformed from 'Stalin to Mr Bean' during his time as prime minister. Ministers face similar question-and-answer sessions within their own area of responsibility.

The vote of confidence

A vote of confidence, or no-confidence motion, is a formal vote taken in the Commons in response to the tabling of a motion that the Commons has no confidence in the government of the day. By convention, the prime minister of a government losing such a vote should request the dissolution of Parliament and a general election. Though a government is unlikely to lose a vote of confidence when it holds a clear Commons majority, minority administrations and governments possessing wafer-thin Commons majorities can fall should opposition parties mobilise and vote en masse. James Callaghan's Labour government lost a vote of confidence in 1979, a defeat that prompted the 1979 general election and 18 years in opposition for the Labour Party.

Early day motions and topical debates

Early day motions call for a Commons debate on a named issue. MPs can propose and add their names to such motions and thereby raise their concerns with govern-ment. Though there is often little time for the issues raised to be debated formally, it provides one more way in which constituents' grievances can be vented through their elected representatives. The Commons also holds topical debates on matters of public interest. Opposition parties are given some time to initiate debates on topics that are of interest to them.

The Commons Liaison Committee

Although Commons committees do not have the power to subpoena (i.e. force) witnesses to appear before them, Tony Blair when prime minister did agree to appear before the Commons Liaison Committee twice each year. This committee, which comprises the chairs of the various Commons departmental select committees, meets at Portcullis House in the Boothroyd Committee Room. Although fairly infrequent, these meetings have provided a genuine opportunity for MPs to question the prime minister outside of the theatre that is PMQs. In the February 2006 session, for example, the prime minister was quizzed on issues as varied as the UK's presidencies of the G8 and the EU, the government's reform agenda for healthcare and schools, relations with Iran and the likely fallout from elections in Palestine.

Frontbenchers

Frontbenchers are those members of Parliament who hold senior positions in govern-ment, act as shadow ministers for the official opposition, or are spokespeople for other parties. The term refers to the fact that such individuals occupy the front benches in the Commons. Their role as spokesperson for their party on a particular area of policy means that frontbenchers will often be heavily involved at ministers' questions, PMQs and when legislation relevant to their area of responsibility is being introduced or debated in the chamber. Government legislation is normally introduced formally to Parliament by the relevant minister, who will obviously be a frontbencher.

The official opposition

The party that secures the second highest number of seats in the Commons following a general election is referred to as the official opposition. The shadow cabinet is drawn from the leading figures on that party's front bench. The official opposition receives public money (known as 'short money' after the former Leader of the Commons, Edward Short) to help cover the costs of holding the government of the day to account. The leader of the opposition alone was given £647,122 to help cover the costs of running his office in the financial year beginning 1 April 2008. The opposition is also able to act as a check on the government through its use of opposition days, when it can determine the topic of debate. Under House of Commons Standing Order SO14 (2), 20 such days are available to opposition parties in each session; 17 are at the disposal of the leader of the official opposition, with 3 allocated to the second largest opposition party.

Backbenchers

The term 'backbencher' refers to all those MPs who sit on the backbenches — who do not hold frontbench responsibilities in their party as ministers, shadow ministers or party spokesperson on a given issue. Whereas those on the front benches have a number of additional demands on their time, backbenchers should in theory be able to focus entirely on the task of representing their constituents. In reality, however, all MPs have to contend with a number of conflicting demands on their time and loyalty.

The four roles of an MP

(1) **Representative:** MPs play an important role in representing the interests of constituents facing problems at home or abroad. Most MPs hold regular surgeries, where they meet constituents and gauge local opinion.

(2) **Loyal party drone:** most MPs are elected by virtue of the party label that they carry during the election, rather than as a result of any personal appeal. It could therefore be said that logically MPs should 'toe the line' once in Parliament. Party whips serve to enforce discipline by offering or withholding promotion to government, or threatening to withdraw the whip, leaving MPs vulnerable to de-selection in their constituencies.

(3) **Watchdog:** traditionally MPs within Parliament have had the role of holding government to account through the various debates, committees, PMQs and minister's questions. There have always been MPs who prioritise this role (Tony Benn and Dennis Skinner, for example).

(4) **Legislator:** for a bill to become an Act it must be passed through the House of Commons. As a result MPs ultimately have the power to kill government legislation — though in reality this rarely even comes close to happening.

A bill introduced by an MP who does not hold a government position is commonly referred to as a Private Member's Bill. Though the government's domination of the available time in Parliament means that such bills only rarely find their way onto the statute books, a number of significant pieces of legislation originated as Private Member's Bills, e.g. the Abortion Act (1967). Private Member's Bills are normally introduced by those drawing high lots in a ballot of MPs (a 'ballot bill') or under the Ten Minute Rule.

The rise of 'career politicians'

Many writers have charted the rise of career politicians in the House of Commons. Whereas MPs in the 1940s served an average of only 5 years, today's MPs often linger for 15 or 20 years. The job has clearly changed in recent times, making it a far more attractive option. Salaries and allowances have improved, the working hours have become more sociable and many MPs now have far more comfortable offices in Portcullis House (see the box below).

MP salary and allowances (April 2008)

Salary	£61,820
Staffing allowance	£100,205
Incidental Expenses Provision (IEP)	£22,193
IT equipment (centrally provided)	£3,000
London supplement	£2,916
Additional costs allowance	£24,005
Communications allowance	£10,400

Source: House of Commons Research Paper 08/31

An individual's desire to secure and then retain such a position at all costs is likely to lead to greater party loyalty within the chamber. Such changes have also resulted in an increase in the number of MPs who enter the chamber with no prior career outside of the world of politics. The elevation of former special advisors to the Commons reflects this trend, e.g. David Miliband.

The role and influence of the party whips

The role of the government whips is to ensure that the government maintains a majority in votes taken in Parliament. The chief whip attends cabinet meetings and has the status of a senior minister.

Whips are commonly said to employ a 'carrot and stick' approach, offering the lure of promotion to government office for those who are loyal and the threat of a life on the back benches — or worse — for those who go against the party whip. John Major's meteoric rise to the post of prime minister (see below) was often said to be as much a result of his unerring loyalty in the Commons as it was to his inherent abilities.

John Major: 10 steps to Number 10

1979	Became an MP
1981	Parliamentary Private Secretary, serving in the Home Office
1983	Assistant Whip
1984	Treasury Whip
1985	Under Secretary of State for Social Security
1986	Minister of State for Social Security
1987	Chief Secretary to the Treasury
1989 (July)	Foreign Secretary
1989 (October)	Chancellor of the Exchequer
1990 (November)	Prime Minister

The whips' ultimate sanction is to **remove the whip** from an MP. This effectively throws the MP out of the parliamentary party and leaves him/her vulnerable to de-selection in the constituency. This sanction is used only rarely as it has the capacity to damage the parliamentary party as much as it does the individual concerned. In 1994 under John Major, however, eight Conservative MPs (later dubbed the 'whipless wonders') had the whip withdrawn for disloyalty over votes relating to the provisions of the Maastricht Treaty.

Some MPs choose to resign the whip or even to cross the floor of the House and join another party by taking that party's whip. They can do this without seeking re-election because — in theory — they as individuals are elected, not the party.

The term 'whip' is also used to refer to the weekly document that each party produces, detailing business in Parliament and indicating the way in which the said party expects its MPs to vote. Items underlined three times (a 'three-line-whip') are those where the party demands the MP to attend and vote in a particular way as regards the division in question.

The core executive

Relations within the core executive, the PM and cabinet

What is the core executive?

Although the debate over precisely where power lies within the executive has often focused on the relationship between the prime minister and cabinet, it has become increasingly common for commentators to try to put PM–cabinet relations into context by considering the part played by other individuals and bodies within the core executive.

According to R. A. W. Rhodes, 'the term core executive refers to all those organisations and procedures which coordinate central government policies, and act as final arbiters of conflict between different parts of the government machine'. He continues:

> In brief, the core executive is the heart of the machine, covering the complex web of institutions, networks and practices surrounding the prime minister, cabinet, cabinet committees and their official counterparts, less formalised ministerial 'clubs' or meetings, bilateral negotiations and interdepartmental committees. It also includes coordinating departments, chiefly the Cabinet Office, the Treasury, the Foreign Office, the law officers, and the security and intelligence services.

> Source: 'From Prime Ministerial Power to Core Executive', R. A. W. Rhodes and P. Dunleavy, *Prime Minister, Cabinet and Core Executive* (Macmillan, 1995)

The prime minister: roles, powers and resources

Origins of the office of prime minister

The office of prime minister is based largely upon convention. In the reign of George I (1714–27), the monarch stopped attending cabinet meetings, partly because he spoke poor English. At that time, the First Lord of the Treasury began chairing cabinet meetings, thereby becoming the prime minister — the king's representative in cabinet. Modern prime ministers still retain the formal title of First Lord of the Treasury.

Though the role of prime minister emerged in the 1720s, one would be wrong to think that prime ministerial power developed in a straight line from that point to the present. George III, for example, tried to reassert royal power by replacing the Fox–North coalition with William Pitt the Younger in 1783. That said, even Queen Victoria, who did not conform to the traditional model of a constitutional monarch, was effectively forced to appoint William Gladstone as prime minister again in 1880, because he led the party that had the best chance of commanding a majority in the Commons.

Early prime ministers

Although Robert Walpole is generally regarded as the first prime minister (1721–42), many see Robert Peel (1841–46) as the first modern prime minister. The title of prime minister was not formally used until Benjamin Disraeli signed the Treaty of Berlin (1878) as the prime minister of England.

Sources of prime ministerial power

The powers of the PM, like the role itself, have evolved gradually, largely as a result of the assimilation of **royal prerogative** powers. As the power of the monarch declined to a point where even Walter Bagehot was able to refer to it as a 'dignified' (i.e. ceremonial) part of the constitution, the role of prime minister developed to fill the vacuum.

There are three sources of prime ministerial power.

(1) Powers formally assigned to the monarch under the royal prerogative, but now exercised by the prime minister on the monarch's behalf

The term 'royal prerogative' is usually applied to those powers once held by the monarch in common law. Through the passing of parliamentary statute and the emergence of new conventions, most of these powers have now been transferred either in law or in practice to the prime minister or to Parliament. The ability of the prime minister to assimilate prerogative powers since the turn of the eighteenth century has been a key feature of the development of the office. Prerogative powers include the ability to control the armed forces, declare war, make treaties, annex and cede territory, exercise patronage, and control the workings of the civil service.

(2) Powers that have emerged through convention

Though the assimilation of prerogative powers has been the most significant process by which the UK prime minister's position has been defined and extended, one should not underestimate the extent to which the office has developed through convention. It is, after all, by convention rather than under statute that many of the prerogative powers have passed into the hands of the premier. It is also through convention that citizens, party, parliament, cabinet and key officials have come to submit themselves to prime ministerial authority, to a greater or lesser extent.

(3) Powers based upon the prime minister's role as leader of the majority party in the House of Commons

Another crucial convention is that the leader of the majority party in the Commons is offered the job of prime minister by the monarch following a general election — and that the same individual will lose this position in the event that his/her government loses the confidence of the chamber. This convention, together with the development of coherent and disciplined parties since the 1850s, has provided a key source of prime ministerial power and authority. The importance of this link between the post of prime minister and that of party leader is emphasised by the fact that those forced to give up the leadership of their party (e.g. Margaret Thatcher in 1990) must also give up the keys to Number 10. The prime minister's power and authority rests, therefore, upon the confidence of the Commons, which, in a majority government, is in turn dependent upon the confidence and support of those sitting on his/her own benches.

Roles of the prime minister

The absence of a codified constitution formally detailing the prime minister's various roles and powers has inevitably led commentators to formulate their own lists. Such uncertainty over the roles performed by the premier is not unique to the UK system. Even in the USA, where presidents are formally assigned the role of chief executive in Article II of the Constitution, other roles — for example those of 'chief legislator' and *de facto* 'head of state' — have developed over time through convention.

In essence the roles of the modern prime minister are five-fold:

(1) chief executive

(2) chief legislator

(3) chief diplomat

(4) public relations chief

(5) party chief

Powers of the prime minister

When discharging these roles the PM has at his/her disposal a range of powers.

(1) Powers of patronage

One aspect of the prime minister's role as *de facto* chief executive is considerable powers of patronage. For example, he/she has the power to:

- appoint and dismiss ministers at cabinet level and below
- appoint senior civil servants (including senior diplomats, members of quangos and special advisors, heads of nationalised industries)
- appoint bishops in the Church of England
- create peers
- appoint senior judges (prior to the Constitutional Reform Act (2005))
- nominate individuals for the honours list

(2) Powers over cabinet, government and the civil service

Though the prime minister's power over the cabinet is greatly enhanced by his/her ability to promote or demote political allies and potential rivals (the power to 'hire and fire'), the premier's powers over cabinet, government and civil service do not stop there. The PM also controls:

- the number, timing and duration of cabinet meetings
- cabinet agendas and minutes — the PM can 'take the feeling of the meeting', without holding a formal vote in cabinet
- the conduct of meetings and who speaks when
- the structure and composition of cabinet committees
- the make-up and organisation of the government in a broader sense, i.e. the 80 or so government posts which are not cabinet rank
- appointments to and the operation of the higher levels of the civil service

(3) Powers over Parliament

The PM has considerable power as the leader of the majority party in the Commons. He/she controls the parliamentary timetable and can impose the government's agenda. The PM is the public face of party and government, controlling key appointments within the party as well as within government.

The PM can rely on a degree of party loyalty simply by virtue of the fact that the party is in government. When 'backs are against the wall', the PM can even threaten to ask the Queen to dissolve Parliament and call an election as a means of forcing rebels from his/her own party into line. This was a tactic adopted by John Major over a number of votes relating to the Maastricht Treaty in 1993 and 1994.

(4) Power over the agenda

As we have seen, the prime minister's control of the executive and his/her ability to control Parliament through powers of patronage and as party leader give the incumbent a key role in agenda setting and policy-making. It is, after all, the prime minister who is largely responsible for the Queen's Speech, and the measures outlined at the state opening of Parliament are normally approved by the PM in their entirety. This ability to set the political agenda has been enhanced by the rise of the mass media and the extent to which the media focuses on the premier.

(5) Powers on the world stage

The prime minister's position as world leader is rooted in the prerogative powers to make war and conclude treaties, but is has been enhanced by the rise of the mass media.

Limitations (or constraints) on prime ministerial power

(1) Limited by the cabinet

Although no formal mechanism exists by which the cabinet can remove the prime minister, it can still provide a meaningful check on prime ministerial power. The seniority of colleagues within one's party might demand their inclusion in cabinet (e.g. Jack Straw in 1997), as might a need for ideological balance (e.g. John Prescott in 1997), or a need to reward those who have supported one's rise to the position of prime minister (e.g. Gordon Brown in 1997). There are also questions of availability for office, ability and relevant experience. If the PM excludes or forces out key figures they can often become dangerous enemies on the back benches, e.g. Michael Heseltine under Thatcher, or Mo Mowlam, Clare Short and Robin Cook under Blair.

Abuse of the PM's powers in cabinet can also bring criticism (e.g. Mo Mowlam accusing Blair of 'control freakery'). Some issues demand inclusion on the cabinet agenda, with failure to concede leading to embarrassing cabinet resignations (e.g. Heseltine in 1995 over Westland) or threats of resignation (e.g. Geoffrey Howe and Nigel Lawson's threat to resign from Margaret Thatcher's cabinet over the issue of UK entry to the Exchange Rate Mechanism in June 1989).

Though prime ministers clearly have the powers necessary to take the initiative within cabinet meetings, an overly domineering approach can be counterproductive in the long run. Prime ministers who pursue specific policies in the face of serious opposition within the broader cabinet and/or parliamentary party can face significant difficulties if these policies fail, e.g. Thatcher and the Poll Tax, Blair over weapons of mass destruction (WMD) and Iraq.

(2) Limited by Parliament

Though Parliament rarely rejects or seriously amends government legislation, it can cause embarrassment, for example through Prime Minister's Questions, debates and motions. *In extremis*, the Commons can force the government to back down (e.g. Gordon Brown's concessions over the removal of the 10% tax rate in 2008) or even remove a government by carrying a vote of no confidence (e.g. Callaghan in 1979).

(3) Limited by party

Failing backbench confidence in Thatcher led to Anthony Meyer's 'stalking horse' leadership challenge in 1989. Michael Heseltine's 1990 leadership challenge ultimately resulted in her resignation. Tony Blair also provoked massive backbench rebellions by pursuing policies that were unpopular with the broader party (e.g. top-up fees) and was effectively forced to pre-announce his departure from office.

(4) Limited by public opinion

The prime minister, along with the whole government, is ultimately accountable to the public through elections. Unpopular prime ministers are more likely to face party leadership challenges, prompted by those backbenchers who fear for their own electoral futures under the incumbent leader. Disappointing opinion poll ratings and bad results in local elections and by-elections can prove particularly damaging to a prime minister's long-term prospects.

(5) Limited by their own abilities and by circumstances

Herbert Asquith famously remarked that 'the office of the prime minister is what its holder chooses and is able to make of it'. Precisely what the incumbent is able to 'make of it' will obviously result from a combination of his/her own abilities, the abilities of others, and the political context — the circumstances in which they hold office. The latter might include the size of the Commons majority, the prevailing economic conditions, or the unexpected. As Harold Macmillan remarked, it is often 'Events, dear boy. Events' that do most to shape a premiership.

The cabinet system

The origins of the cabinet

As is the case with the office of prime minister, the cabinet has evolved over time. In English usage, the term 'cabal' originated as an acronym for the core of ministers under Charles II who ran the government from 1668: **C**lifford; **A**rlington; **B**uckingham; **A**shley; and **L**auderdale. It is from this body that the modern cabinet is said to have evolved.

In the reign of George I (1714–27), when the monarch stopped attending cabinet meetings, the body was chaired by the First Lord of the Treasury — and this formal title is still retained by modern prime ministers. In the nineteenth century, the extension of the franchise and the emergence of a more formal party system resulted in cabinets relying on the support of the Commons and, therefore, on the majority party in the Commons. It is from this point that notions of single party government and collective responsibility emerged.

By the latter half of the nineteenth century the cabinet was seen as the engine room of government. By 1867, for example, Walter Bagehot was describing it as a 'hyphen' or 'buckle' that linked the executive part of government to the legislature. The prime minister was merely *primus inter pares* ('first among equals').

> The cabinet, in a word, is a board of control chosen by the legislature, out of persons whom it trusts and knows, to rule the nation...A cabinet is a combining committee, — a *hyphen* which joins, a *buckle* which fastens, the legislative part of the state to the executive part of the state. In its origin it belongs to the one, in its functions it belongs to the other.
>
> Walter Bagehot, *The English Constitution* (1867)

The composition of the cabinet

Cabinet organisation

In 2008 the cabinet consisted of 22 paid members and fulfilled a number of important functions. As we have seen, the prime minister controls the cabinet through his/her powers of patronage and his/her ability to control the number, timing, duration and style of meetings. The PM also sets the agenda and takes the feeling of meetings.

Cabinet committees

Committees are generally chaired by the PM or other senior cabinet colleagues determined by the premier. Remaining members are drawn from the cabinet as appropriate. Committees generally fall into various categories: foreign and defence, domestic/home affairs, and economic. The full cabinet has increasingly become a body for airing and rubber-stamping decisions taken at committee. Crucially, the principle of **collective responsibility** extends to those decisions taken in committee as well as those agreed by the full cabinet. This means that even cabinet members who are not attending the committee making a particular decision will still be required to stand by it publicly.

The Cabinet Office (CO)

The CO is the key player in coordinating the activities of government. Strengthened by Labour in 2001, the office comprised 2,000 staff, including a CO minister, the cabinet secretary, four secretariats (economic/domestic, defence/overseas, European, constitution), and a range of other bodies such as the Performance and Innovation Unit.

Labour's changes also saw a physical centralisation of the CO, with staff from around 17 former CO buildings relocated to new offices in Downing Street. This reorganisation of the CO and the extent to which it has become intertwined with the Prime Minister's Office, establishing a virtual Prime Minister's Department, is said to pose a major threat to cabinet government. These developments are dealt with more fully in Chapter 3 of *The Prime Minister & the Cabinet* by Paul Fairclough (Philip Allan Updates).

The roles and functions of cabinet and cabinet ministers

The traditional view is that decision-making power within government rests with the cabinet, with the prime minister merely acting as 'chair' (*primus inter pares*):

- Cabinet is a collective decision-making body.
- Cabinet operates under the doctrine of collective responsibility — those present agree to stand by the decisions made in closed sessions.

(1) Decision-making

Cabinet was once seen as the key decision-making body, what Bagehot called the 'efficient secret' of British government — the 'buckle' that joined the executive part of the state to the legislature. The cabinet's role in this area has, however, been undermined by the development of prime ministerial power and the increased use of bilaterals. Key decisions may now be taken elsewhere and presented to the cabinet as a *fait accompli*, e.g. the decisions over the Millennium Dome and handing control over interest rates to the Bank of England in 1997.

(2) Coordinating departments

Cabinet has always had a role in coordinating the activities of government departments. While the decision-making role of cabinet has diminished somewhat, its position as an arena where individuals can report on their activities and bring colleagues up to speed is still crucial.

(3) Forward planning

Cabinet retains a role in addressing problems arising from policy and/or events. Cabinet provides a 'talking shop' where the direction of policy can, if necessary, be discussed and where the broad direction of policy can be re-focused. It is also a place where ministers can raise genuine concerns and deal with contingency (i.e. unexpected events or emergencies).

Changes to the operation of cabinet under Blair

From 1997, Labour under Tony Blair made significant changes to cabinet working practices, reducing full cabinet meetings to a single, 45-minute session each week. Moreover, those meetings that did take place were regarded with little more than contempt by many departing cabinet ministers. Mo Mowlam, for example, felt that Blair had reduced the cabinet to the status of a briefing room where colleagues were brought up to speed on policies already decided elsewhere in bilateral meetings or other less formal settings. Mowlam and others used the term 'sofa government' to describe Blair's approach to decision-making. Blair's biographer, Anthony Seldon, used the term 'denocracy' — a reference to Blair's preference for making decisions following informal meetings in the 'den' at Number 10.

Different models of executive control

Cabinet government

The PM is merely *primus inter pares* ('first among equals'). Cabinet is a decision-making body, operating under collective responsibility.

Reasons for the decline of cabinet government are:
- The increase in the scope and complexity of government activity.
- The emergence and subsequent rise of cabinet committees.
- The tendency towards the use of bilateral meetings and other less formal arrangements over full cabinet meetings.
- The increase in the authority and status afforded to the prime minister.
- The behaviour of cabinet members.

Prime ministerial cliques/'kitchen cabinet'

The PM works closely with a clique of key advisors. Membership of this clique would be fairly fixed but other individuals might be brought into the circle on certain issues. The full cabinet is merely a rubber stamp.

Departmentalised government

Individual government departments have control over their respective areas and ministers act with a degree of autonomy. The PM bows to departmental expertise but holds ministers accountable for their decisions. Cabinet becomes an arena for interdepartmental coordination.

Differentiated/segmented decisions

The degree of prime ministerial dominance varies in different policy areas. The PM might dominate the heights of government — foreign policy, defence, key economic policy decisions — whereas the cabinet might be given a high degree of autonomy in other areas.

Prime ministerial government

This was identified by writers such as Richard Crossman in the 1960s and Tony Benn in the 1980s. Though talk of prime ministerial government and what Lord Hailsham referred to as the 'elective dictatorship' still persists in the media, the debate has moved on somewhat in recent years with the suggestion that the prime minister has become a *de facto* president.

Do we have prime ministerial or presidential government in Britain?

As Michael Foley observed in *The Rise of the British Presidency* (1993), 'The *premier-ship*, which has become an increasingly conventional term, is itself replete with suggestions of a singular office in form and substance.' This notion of a **'singular office'** inevitably leads to comparisons being drawn between the UK prime minister and the US president. We should recognise, however, that the situation as regards the prime minister is a uniquely British one because of the way in which his or her powers originate — not in the limited ('checked') powers available to the US president under a codified constitution, but through the assimilation of the unchecked prerogative powers formally exercised by the monarch. Whereas talk of a 'presidential prime minister' appears, therefore, to suggest an increase in power, the US president's powers are in fact clearly circumscribed by the constitutional checks and balances instituted by the Founding Fathers.

In reality, the prime minister — whether by virtue of his/her position as leader of the majority party in the Commons or through the exercise of prerogative powers — has a good deal more room for manoeuvre than the US counterpart in virtually every area of operation. Some commentators have addressed this paradox by attempting to draw comparisons between the prime minister and the French president. As Richard Rose argues, 'the *Palais de l'Eysée* is a constitutional "halfway" house between Number 10 and the White House, since France has a Parliament and a prime minister as well as a president.'

'Presidencies' compared: the UK, France and the USA

	Britain	**France**	**USA**
Media visibility	High	High	High
Route to top	Parliament	Civil service	Governor
Election	Party	Popular	Popular
Term	Insecure	Fixed: 7 years	Fixed: 4 years
Constitution	Unitary	Unitary	Federal
Checks	Slight, informal	*Cohabitation*	Congress, Supreme Court
Domestic policy	High	High	So-so
International policy	EU member	EU member	Super

Source: adapted from Richard Rose, *The Prime Minister in a Shrinking World* (Polity, 2001)

Though such debate is interesting, it is also something of a side issue, as the presidential thesis is rooted more in style and approach than it is in substance. Rather than spending too much time seeking parallels with other systems, we should focus instead on those features that have been said to characterise what is, as we have already noted, a uniquely British presidency.

Foley's thesis identifies four characteristics which — in his view — justify the notion that the UK is moving towards a presidential system. Some of these themes were echoed in the work of writers such as Richard Rose, whose book *The Prime Minister in a Shrinking World* (2001), painted a picture of a premier transformed by the role he was required to take on the world stage.

(1) **Spatial leadership:** the tendency for prime ministers to try to create visible distance between themselves and the machinery of government.

(2) **Cult of the outsider:** the tendency for prime ministers to characterise themselves as 'outsiders', fighting against formal structures and challenging 'business as usual'.

(3) **Public leadership:** the way in which prime ministers have sought to appeal directly to the public through the modern mass media, thereby circumventing the normal channels.

(4) **The personal factor:** the way in which prime ministers have become 'expanded personalities', personifying 'mass demands, common anxieties, social hopes and national ideals'.

Source: Michael Foley, 'Presidential Politics in Britain', *Talking Politics* Vol. 6.3. Summer 1994

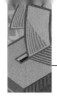

Policy-making and implementation

The organisation of government departments

Departmental hierarchy

Government departments (e.g. Treasury, Foreign Office, Transport) consist of a number of ministers of varying rank, working alongside civil servants.

Each government department is headed by a secretary of state. Below secretaries of state there are two ranks of junior ministers (ministers of state and parliamentary under-secretaries) and private parliamentary secretaries. All three non-cabinet ranks serve as testing grounds for those with potential.

Case study: Department of Transport (February 2008)

Ministerial hierarchy	A minister's responsibilities
• Ruth Kelly MP (Secretary of State for Transport) • **Rosie Winterton MP** (Minister of State and Minister for Yorkshire and the Humber) • Jim Fitzpatrick MP (Parliamentary Under-Secretary of State) • Tom Harris MP (Parliamentary Under-Secretary of State)	**Rosie Winterton MP** Minister of State for Transport Responsible for: • Regional transport strategy • Local public transport • Walking, cycling and sustainable transport • Local roads and traffic • Access and equality • Europe

Collective responsibility and individual ministerial responsibility

Traditionally, cabinet ministers have been expected to work under the twin doctrines of collective responsibility and individual ministerial responsibility — though in recent years both doctrines appear to have declined somewhat.

Collective responsibility demands that members of the cabinet publicly stand by those decisions made collectively within cabinet. Those who are not prepared to do so are expected to resign their post and argue their case from the backbenches, e.g. Robin Cook's resignation over Iraq in 2001.

Individual ministerial responsibility holds ministers responsible for their own personal conduct (personal responsibility) and the conduct of their departments (role responsibility), requiring them to resign in the event that they fail in either sphere, e.g. Foreign Secretary Lord Carrington's resignation in the wake of the Argentinean invasion of the Falklands in 1981.

The civil service

The civil service is the **administrative** or **bureaucratic** arm of government; its members are technically servants of the Crown. Civil servants have traditionally been divided into those who work on specific areas of policy (in departmental groups and agencies) and those who work across the service — service-wide generalists or service-wide specialists (e.g. statisticians). The top four grades within the senior civil service (c.1,000 staff) have traditionally held the greatest input into policy.

Civil service reform (1979–2005)

The civil service was often criticised for being inefficient and obstructive. In recent years it has been affected by two key developments:

(1) The 'hiving-off' of many responsibilities to semi-autonomous agencies (called 'executive agencies' or '**Next Steps agencies**').

(2) The rise of **special advisers** (sometimes called 'spin doctors').

Some argue that such changes have resulted in the **politicisation** of the service, which threatens its traditional principles of impartiality, anonymity and permanence.

The Fulton Report (1968) criticised the civil service's amateurish approach. Though Fulton's proposals were never fully implemented, the service underwent major changes between 1979 and 1990 under Margaret Thatcher. Derek Rayner's Efficiency Unit led to the Financial Management Initiative (FMI), which sought to introduce a more business-like culture to the service. Civil service staff numbers fell from 750,000 in 1979 to 600,000 in 1990.

The Next Steps Programme (from 1988) resulted in a process of agencification. By 1990, 75% of all civil servants were employed by such agencies. John Major's Citizen's Charter (1991) emphasised the importance of quality in public services and was largely retained by Labour from 1997. Labour also emphasised the need for greater forward planning and a less risk-averse culture in the civil service.

The impact of agencification

Agencification is the process of hiving-off government services into semi-autonomous agencies. It has resulted in some civil servants becoming publicly known and identified as being responsible for the execution of policy (e.g. the head of the Child Support Agency). Public servants may even be forced to resign over policy failures. This undermines traditional civil service principles of impartiality, anonymity and permanence as well as the doctrine of individual ministerial responsibility.

In April 1990 there were 12 agencies. By 2005 there were around 130, employing 75% of all civil servants (e.g. the Home Office works alongside HM Prison Service, the Identity and Passport Service and the Forensic Science Service).

Characteristics and roles of the civil service

Civil service principles

Government departments are staffed by civil servants appointed by the Crown. All civil servants were traditionally said to operate under three interlocking principles:

(1) Impartiality

Theory: civil servants serve the Crown and should not be asked to perform party political functions.

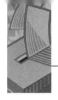

Practice: impartiality has been undermined by the rise of special advisers and by the politicisation of the service since 1979.

(2) Anonymity

Theory: individual civil servants should not be identified publicly as the source of policy, due in part to the doctrine of ministerial responsibility.

Practice: anonymity has been undermined by public criticism of named civil servants over policy (e.g. over the Westland Affair in 1986) and by the rise of agencies where civil servants and not ministers appear to be responsible for policy (e.g. the Prison Service).

(3) Permanence

Theory: civil servants should remain in office even following a change in government.

Practice: many civil servants (heads of agencies, special advisers) are now on fixed-term contracts. This serves to undermine permanence.

Confidentiality?

Some argue that a fourth principle, that of confidentiality, could be added to the three commonly ascribed to the UK civil service. In theory, civil servants were traditionally bound by the Official Secrets Act. They could neither choose to reveal their advice, nor be forced to do so. In reality, leaks and other events have served to undermine this principle as well. Examples include:

- Sarah Tisdall was sentenced to 6 months' imprisonment in 1983 for leaking details of the arrival of cruise missiles at Greenham Common.
- Clive Ponting was acquitted in 1985 of leaking details relating to the sinking of the Argentinean battleship the *General Belgrano* during the Falklands War.
- David Shayler was sentenced to 6 months' imprisonment in 2002 for leaking information relating to MI5 operations.

Role of the civil service

Although far more has been written regarding civil service principles, it is possible to identify a number of distinct roles:

Research

The civil service is the engine room of government. Its specialists provide the detailed research essential to policy formation, a crucial role when most ministers are generalists.

Policy advice

The 1,000 top bureaucrats in the senior civil service still play a crucial role in advising ministers and presenting proposals at the minister's request.

Policy execution

The civil service plays a crucial role in executing (i.e. implementing) government policy. Much of this work is now done with government agencies.

Departmental administration
The civil service is responsible for the organisation of each government department (e.g. record keeping).

Ensuring continuity and a smooth transition between governments
The civil service provides continuity in departments through ministerial reshuffles and changes in government. This role is made possible due to the civil service principles of impartiality, anonymity, and permanence.

The relationship between ministers and civil servants

Models of ministerial–civil service relations
In his article 'Ministers and Mandarins' (*Talking Politics*, Vol. 4, No. 2, 1991), Kevin Theakston outlined four models of ministerial–civil servant relationship.

(1) Formal constitutional model
Civil servants serve ministers, providing information but preserving impartiality, anonymity and, therefore, permanence.

(2) Adversarial model
Ministers and civil servants are engaged in a struggle for power. The civil service has its own agenda and seeks to obstruct government.

(3) Village life in the Whitehall community model
Ministers within the department provide the vision and drive; the civil servants fill in the detail based upon their knowledge and experience of what has worked in the past.

(4) Bureaucratic expansionism model
Civil servants serve their own interests by creating bureaucratic empires that are financially inefficient and get in the way of clear and effective government.

Resources of the prime minister, ministers and officials		
Prime minister	**Ministers**	**Officials**
Patronage	Political support	Permanence
Authority	Authority	Knowledge
Political support	Department	Time
Party political support	Knowledge	Whitehall network
Electorate	Policy networks	Control over information
PM's Office	Policy success	Keepers of the constitution
Bilateral policy-making		

Source: adapted from Martin J. Smith, 'The Core Executive', *Politics Review*, September 2000

The UK civil service: servants or masters?

Tony Benn, a Labour minister in the 1970s, felt that the civil service had its own agenda and sought to steer new and inexperienced ministers. This was made easier by the advantages outlined below and by the fact that, as Benn noted in 1981, 'When a government is elected it has maximum energy and minimum knowledge. Just before it is defeated it has maximum knowledge and minimum energy.'

- Civil servants **control information**, denying ministers essential facts or drowning them in paperwork.
- Ministers have **too many other commitments**.
- Top civil servants **outnumber ministers** by 10:1.
- Civil servants can **network**, holding informal (sometimes interdepartmental) meetings that see awkward ministers outmanoeuvred.
- Surrounded by the civil service and cut off from the reality outside their departments, ministers can **'go native'**.
- Top civil servants tend to **'outlive' ministers**, staying in a department a lot longer than the average ministerial term of 2 years.

The 'Yes Minister' model

Though the formal constitutional model characterises the civil service as a body that is there to serve, rather than to govern, many have argued that the control the service exercises over information gives civil servants the upper hand in their relations with ministers.

The BBC comedy *Yes Minister* was based on the career of the hapless fictional Minister for Administrative Affairs (Jim Hacker), who was constantly outwitted by his Permanent Secretary (Sir Humphrey Appleby), despite the best efforts of his Private Secretary (Bernard Woolley). Many observers felt that the relationship between the leading characters was all too realistic.

Special advisers

Most special advisers are civil servants, paid for by the taxpayer. Unlike most regular civil servants, however, they are not bound by the traditional civil service principles. Special advisers are appointed by and tied to the government of the day. They are partisan (i.e. not impartial), often public figures (i.e. not anonymous), and appointed on fixed-term contracts (i.e. not permanent).

Special advisors have two broad roles:
- to make the government less reliant on the work of the civil service
- to help the prime minister keep up-to-date with often far better staffed and resourced government departments

Each cabinet minister has traditionally been able to appoint two special advisers, in addition to those serving the PM. In the 1980s and 1990s some lower-ranking ministers also started to appoint such individuals. Labour made extensive use of special advisers from 1997. By 2003 there were 108 (27 prime ministerial advisers and 81 government advisers), compared to just 5 in 1990, e.g. Jonathon Powell (Blair's Chief of Staff) and Alastair Campbell (ultimately Director of Communications).

'Spin doctors'

Special advisers, or 'spin doctors' as they increasingly became known following Labour's election to office in 1997, often face criticism for the way in which they appear to serve a party-political function while — in many cases — being funded by the taxpayer. A number of high-profile scandals involving high-level special advisers in the late 1990s, and the party's apparent obsession with staying 'on-message', led some broadsheets to suggest that the party was 'spinning out of control'.

Problems over policy, spin, and departmental management at the Department of Transport eventually led to the departure of three key figures in 2002:

- **Jo Moore:** Stephen Byers' media advisor, who on 9/11 was said to have sent an e-mail around the department suggesting that it was a 'good day to bury bad news'.
- **Martin Sixsmith:** the civil servant in charge of departmental communications.
- **Stephen Byers:** the Secretary of State for Transport.

Multi-level governance

Elected local and devolved government in the UK

The main powers of elected local government

Local government is largely at the mercy of central government. The UK remains a **unitary state** and the Westminster Parliament has the ultimate power to control local government through a number of means:

- **Finance:** through controlling the level of central government grant. Central government can also cap the levels of local taxation.
- **Legislation:** central government has the power to extend or limit the range and extent of local government activities by statute or through delegated legislation. If it wanted to it could abolish local government outright.
- **Inspections:** central government can inspect the delivery of local government services directly, or through organisations such as OFSTED.
- **The doctrine of *ultra vires*:** local authorities are only allowed to do what is authorised by law. Anything else is *ultra vires* (beyond their authority). Individual councillors can be fined (surcharged) to pay for the costs incurred in pursuing such policies.
- **Acting in default:** ultimately, central government can act in default, taking a particular local service under the direct control of central government.

Ultra vires and default

During the 1980s, faced with an extended period of Conservative government at Westminster, many Labour-controlled councils in urban areas sought to pursue a socialist agenda at local level. This co-called **municipal socialism** provoked legal action and threats of default proceedings in a number of areas.

- In 1982 Norwich City Council went all the way to the High Court in protest at then Environment Secretary Michael Heseltine's implementation of the right to buy legislation — though it lost. The council's unwillingness to sell its council housing stock led to threats of default proceedings.
- In 1985 several councillors on the Labour-controlled Liverpool City Council were surcharged £106,000, having set an illegal deficit budget. They included Derek Hatton, the Deputy Leader of the Council, who was expelled from the Labour Party the following year as part of Neil Kinnock's purge on members of the 'outlawed' militant tendency.

Local government finance

Though the lion's share of local government revenue is still provided by the central government revenue grant and nationally distributed business rates, it is the issue of local taxation that remains the most controversial:

- First, because it comes as a highly visible annual bill and must be met from disposable income, rather than being deducted from income at source or taken less visibly through indirect taxes (e.g. VAT).
- Second, because people do not really understand what local taxation is for.

For example, in 2005–06 the income received by Leicestershire County Council comprised:

- government revenue grant: £165.9 m
- business rates: £188.5 m
- local taxation (council tax): £191.0 m

The changing face of local government taxation

The rates

Until 1989 all UK local authorities levied rates. This was a property-based tax, under which the owner of each property was charged an annual tax based upon the size and standard of the property. This tax penalised elderly single people living in large houses.

Community charge ('Poll Tax')

The Poll Tax, so-called because everyone over 18 was eligible, was introduced in 1990 in England and Wales (1989 in Scotland). The Conservatives argued that by making everyone pay the same amount, the policy would make local authorities more accountable for the services provided. Citizens would, it was argued, take more interest in local government.

Council tax

The unprecedented opposition to the Poll Tax — in the form of mass demonstrations, non-registration and non-payment — contributed to Margaret Thatcher's demise in 1990. New Environment Secretary Michael Heseltine announced plans to scrap the tax in 1991 and council tax was introduced in 1993. This was a property-based tax — like the rates — but with significant concessions for those who were living alone or less able to pay. Despite this, council tax remains extremely contentious.

Local government evaluated

The debate over local government usually focuses on the extent to which it continues to serve a useful function within the UK system. Regardless of its merits and demerits, however, it is inevitable that some form of local government will persist, not least because of the existing pressures on the Westminster government.

Arguments for and against local government

Political participation	
+	The existence of local government encourages people to get involved in making the decisions that will affect them the most
−	Participation rates in local government are extremely low and voter turnout is poor
Representation	
+	Local government can represent local people more effectively than Westminster
−	Councillors rarely have the resources or the time to represent local people properly. Local government is amateurish
Relevance	
+	Local councils know what the local area needs. It makes sense to delegate power
−	Local governments often get lost in the detail and fail to see the bigger picture. Central government can often be more objective and, therefore, more appropriate

The powers of the Scottish Parliament and Welsh Assembly

The Scottish Parliament

In the referendum of March 1979, Scots voted in favour of a devolved Parliament (51% to 48.4%), but the terms of the vote stated that there needed to be support from 40% of the electorate for the plans to go ahead. With turnout at only 63.8%, the 'yes' camp fell short of the margin required. In September 1997 a second referendum ran on the basis of a simple majority of those voting — i.e. without the 40% threshold that had caused the 1979 proposal to fall.

The 1997 referendum

The referendum that took place in September 1997 presented the Scottish electorate with two questions: whether there should be a Scottish Parliament; and whether the Parliament should have tax-varying powers. Voters thus had the option of voting 'no, no', 'yes, no' or 'yes, yes' (the latter being the choice of 63.5% of voters).

Function and effectiveness

The Scottish Parliament took **primary legislative control** of areas such as education, agriculture and home affairs. The second 'yes' in the referendum also gave the Parliament **income-tax-varying powers**. The Labour–LibDem coalition administrations from 1999–2005 moved to introduce free long-term nursing care for the elderly, abolish top-up fees, and introduce a more effective Freedom of Information Act. The SNP were the single largest party in the Scottish Parliament after the 2007 elections. They opted to run a minority administration, having failed to find a coalition partner who would commit to a referendum on the issue of Scottish independence.

What is the West Lothian Question?

The phrase 'West Lothian Question' was coined by Enoch Powell in the 1970s as a way of summing up the concerns of the then MP for the Scottish constituency of West Lothian, Tam Dalyell. Dalyell's concerns consisted of two interlocking dilemmas that might result from the programme of devolution planned by the Labour government in the 1970s:

- First, why should MPs representing Scottish, Welsh and Northern Irish constituencies at Westminster be permitted to debate and vote on measures that would no longer affect their own constituents?
- Second, is it right that such MPs would no longer have the ability to vote on matters that did affect their constituents, because such powers had been devolved to — and would therefore be discussed by — separately elected devolved institutions?

The number of Scottish MPs in the Westminster Parliament was reduced from 72 to 59 in the run up to the 2005 general election as a partial remedy to the West Lothian Question.

Particular controversy surrounds Commons votes referred to as 'West Lothian votes', where the majority of English MPs vote against a measure, but it is still passed with the support of MPs representing constituents who are not themselves affected by the Act in question.

'West Lothian votes' under Blair

Bill	Date	All UK MPs		English MPs only		Majority against govt among English MPs
		For govt	Against govt	For govt	Against govt	
Foundation hospitals						
Health and Social Care Bill (2nd Reading)	8.7.03	286	251	217	218	1
Health and Social Care Bill (3rd Reading)	19.11.03	302	285	234	251	17
Top-up fees						
Higher Education Bill (2nd Reading)	27.1.04	316	311	246	261	15
Higher Education Bill (3rd Reading)	31.3.04	316	288	244	246	2

Source: Meg Russell and Guy Lodge, 'Westminster and the English Question', *The Constitution Unit* (2006)

The Welsh Assembly

The referendum of March 1979 saw the Welsh reject the chance to have their own parliament (by 79.7% to 20.3% on a 58.3% turnout). By the time of the 1997 general election, however, the Labour Party was committed to a new referendum — this time on the creation of a Welsh Assembly.

The 1997 referendum

Following its victory in the 1997 general election, the Labour government set the date for the referendums that had been promised on devolution for Scotland and Wales. In the September 1997 vote, the Welsh approved the creation of a Welsh Assembly by 50.3% (559,419 votes) to 49.7% (552,698 votes) — on a 50.1% turnout.

Function and effectiveness

The Assembly was not given the same powers as the Scottish Parliament. It had **no primary legislative powers** but could recommend legislation to the UK Parliament and had a role in overseeing Welsh quangos. It could also implement Westminster legislation in Wales. The Assembly did not have the income-tax-varying powers afforded the Scottish Parliament. In 2004, the Richard Commission recommended that the Assembly should be granted primary legislative powers from 2011 and might also gain tax-varying powers, though such proposals had not been implemented by 2008.

The idea of a unitary state

The UK is traditionally said to be a unitary state as opposed to a federal one. This means that ultimate power in the UK is held by the **central government** at Westminster. Any power that local government or regional government appears to have is merely delegated or 'devolved' to it and can be withdrawn at any time.

Under a federal system, power (sovereignty) is divided between a central government and a number of regions or individual states. Each tier of government has ultimate authority over certain areas of policy, i.e. they have separate spheres of authority or separate jurisdictions. Under a federal system the relationship between the central government and the various states is entrenched — the central government cannot take away the powers of individual states without their consent.

Is the UK still a unitary state?

The biggest challenge to the notion of the UK as a unitary state has been the devolution programme pursued by New Labour since 1997:

- Scottish Parliament and executive
- Welsh Assembly and executive
- Northern Ireland Assembly and executive
- emergence of regional government, e.g. the Greater London Assembly and London Mayor

In addition, some argue that the ongoing process of European integration means that the UK is, in effect, moving towards a situation where it will simply be one 'state' within a 'federal Europe'.

Regardless of such concerns, however, the Westminster Parliament still has the authority and power to withdraw powers that have been devolved or delegated — as was seen with the suspension of power-sharing arrangements in Northern Ireland between 2002 and 2007.

The European Union

Origins

The European Economic Community (EEC) emerged in the 1950s as part of a desire to:

- prevent further wars
- provide economic stability

The European Coal and Steel Community was formed in 1952 by France, Germany, Italy, Belgium, the Netherlands and Luxembourg. In 1957 these six member states signed the Treaty of Rome. This treaty broadened the Coal and Steel Community to include foreign trade and agriculture, thereby creating the EEC. The UK did not join until 1973.

From Economic Community to European Union

By the 1980s the EEC had achieved many of its founding aims — peace in Europe had been preserved for over 35 years and the Common Agricultural Policy had regulated agricultural production through the use of subsidies and quotas.

Many felt that the community needed to set itself new targets. The 1986 Single European Act created a single European market, with free movement of goods, persons, services and capital. The Maastricht Treaty of 1992 took things a stage further, creating the European Union (EU).

Key dates in the emergence of the EU

1952 Coal and Steel Community established

1957 Treaty of Rome — EEC formed

1973 UK (plus Denmark and Ireland) join

1981 Greece joins

1986 Single European Act

1986 Spain and Portugal join

1992 Maastricht Treaty

1995 Austria, Finland and Sweden join

1997 Amsterdam Treaty

2001 Nice Treaty

2004 Accession of 10 more states, bringing the total to 25

2004 EU Constitution agreed

2005 Treaty setting out new EU Constitution abandoned following referendum defeats in France and the Netherlands

2007 Bulgaria and Romania join the EU

2007 Efforts to revise the EU Constitution eventually result in the Lisbon Treaty

2009 Croatia and Macedonia join the EU

The Maastricht Treaty (1992)

While the Single European Act (1986) had deepened the EEC — by allowing for free movement of goods, persons, services and capital across the union — the Maastricht Treaty (1992) widened the scope of the community beyond its origins in economic cooperation, by establishing a European Union founded on three pillars:

- the European community
- justice and home affairs
- foreign and security policy

At the same time, the treaty led to the emergence of the notion of **European citizenship**, and a range of associated rights. In many member states it was argued that people were beginning to see themselves as 'Europeans', above and beyond their national identity.

Common Foreign and Security Policy (CFSP)

The collapse of Yugoslavia in the 1990s and the ongoing problems in the region (e.g. Kosovo) led many to believe that a European-wide peacekeeping or rapid-reaction force might be the best way to deal with problems on the continent. The Maastricht Treaty offered the prospect of some kind of European Defence Force. Germany and France pushed ahead in this area.

Justice and home affairs

The EU was to take an active role in social policy through a series of protocols. The Social Chapter, for example, enshrined wide-ranging EU regulations regarding working conditions and employee entitlements. John Major's signing of the Maastricht Treaty was conditional upon an opt-out from the Social Chapter. Labour adopted most of the Social Chapter after it came to office in 1997, though the UK opt-out from the European Working Time Directive remained.

The Treaty of Amsterdam (1997)

The treaty extended the co-decision procedure into most areas of policy. It also confirmed the incorporation of the Social Chapter into EU treaties (it had previously been a protocol), following the UK's decision to give up the opt-out negotiated by John Major.

The Treaty of Nice (2001)

The treaty focused on the theme of EU enlargement and the resulting reorganisation of EU institutions:

- The extension of the Parliament's co-decision powers into new areas and reapportioning of Parliament seats between member states.
- The restructuring of the European Commission with one commissioner for each member state.
- The reworking of the Council of Ministers' system of qualified majority voting (QMV) to reflect the planned expansion from 15 to 25 EU member states in 2004.

The EU Constitution (2004)

The 2004 enlargement of the EU that resulted from the Treaty of Nice (2001) necessitated a restructuring of key EU institutions. The proposed Constitution, which ran to over 400 pages, sought to bring together the various existing treaties into a single authoritative (codified) document, setting out the rules of the union.

The proposed Constitution did not grant the EU any additional powers, but would have:

- strengthened the role of the European Parliament
- enhanced the role of national parliaments in revising EU law
- extended QMV into 26 policy areas that previously allowed the national veto (e.g. asylum)

Though Tony Blair and others initially argued that the proposed Constitution was merely a 'tidying up exercise', it quickly became apparent that many European citizens took a different view. The French rejection of the treaty to establish the new Constitution in a referendum on 29 May 2005, and the Dutch rejection that followed — again by referendum — on 1 June, resulted in the suspension of the ratification process.

The Lisbon Treaty (2007)

In June 2007 a summit held under the German presidency of the EU resulted in the drafting of the EU Reform Treaty, which was later signed in Lisbon (hence 'the Lisbon Treaty'). This treaty sought to break the 2-year deadlock that had followed the rejection of the 400-page draft EU Constitution by French and Dutch voters in June 2005.

Though the Lisbon Treaty dropped the references to the EU flag and anthem that were present in the 2004 Constitution, other key elements of the Constitution survived largely intact. Valèry Giscard d'Estaing, one of the key architects of the original Constitution, saw the changes between the two documents as 'few and far between...and more cosmetic than real'. The decision to create a post of 'High Representative of the Union for Foreign Affairs and Security Policy' as opposed to that envisaged in the original Constitution of 'Minister of Foreign Affairs', was certainly viewed widely as a change in presentation as opposed to substance.

As a result of negotiations over the new treaty, the UK was able to secure an opt-out in the sphere of justice and home affairs, as well as a separate legally binding protocol preventing the Charter of Fundamental Rights from having full legal force in the UK.

Composition and main powers of key EU institutions

(1) The Council of Ministers and the European Council

The Council of Ministers is the EU's main decision-making body, comprising one minister from each member state. The actual minister involved will depend on the nature of the issues being discussed. A few decisions are still taken on the basis of unanimity but most are now taken under qualified majority voting.

The European Council is a meeting of the EU heads of government, foreign ministers, the Commission President and the Commission Vice-President. The Council is a political rather than legislative body, discussing key issues and setting the EU agenda.

Key term: **intergovernmentalism.** This means cooperation between governments of EU member states without abandoning national interests. The Council of Ministers and the European Council are intergovernmental bodies.

(2) The European Commission

The European Commission is the executive body of the EU, comprising one political appointee from each member state. Commissioners are expected to adopt a supranational attitude. The Commission has the role of initiating legislation and making proposals to the Council and the Parliament. It also acts as the guardian of EU treaties and has the power to execute agreed policies.

Key term: **supra-nationalism.** This means cooperation between governments and their appointees at a level that ignores national interests. The Commission, the Parliament and the Court of Justice are supra-national bodies.

(3) The European Parliament

The European Parliament is the only EU institution that is democratically elected by

The EU Constitution (2004) and Lisbon Treaty (2007) compared

	EU Constitution (2004)	**Lisbon Treaty (2007)**
Form	• Well over 400 pages • Sought to bring together existing treaties into a single authoritative (codified) document that would set out the rules of the Union	• 277 pages • Achieved necessary changes by amending the Treaty of Rome and the Treaty on the European Union (Maastricht), as opposed to creating a new codified 'rule-book' for the EU
The EU presidency	• An EU president elected by the European Council for a single, renewable term of 2½ years. Subject to approval by the EU Parliament	• Provision retained
Council of Ministers' use of qualified majority voting (QMV)	• The use of qualified majority voting to be extended into a number of areas previously requiring unanimity • A qualified vote to be defined as one with at least 55% of the members of the Council (at least 15) and representing member states comprising at least 65% of the EU population. Known as the 'double majority' system	• Provision retained, with this new 'double majority' system to be phased in between 2014 and 2017
The Commission	• To consist of one national from each member state for an initial term of 5 years. Thereafter, a number equal to half of the number of member states	• Retained, with the 'half formula' to be introduced from 2014
The European Parliament	• Extension of co-decision procedure, under which decision-making power is shared between the EU Parliament and the Council of Ministers	• Provision retained
Charter of Fundamental Rights	• Codifies the existing rights and freedoms enjoyed by EU citizens	• Provision retained, without extending the powers of the Union
Foreign and defence policy	• Greater cooperation on foreign affairs and defence • The appointment of a Union Minister of Foreign Affairs to conduct this EU common foreign and security policy	• Provision retained, in essence, but with a 'High Representative of the Union for Foreign Affairs and Security Policy' as opposed to a 'Union Minister of Foreign Affairs'

citizens in each member state. Seats are allocated to individual states in broad proportion to population. Once only advisory, the modern Parliament has legislative powers over certain areas (e.g. the environment) under the so-called co-decision procedure. The Parliament approves the EU budget and confirms the Commission's appointment. Parliamentary censure of the Commission forces its resignation.

Key term: **co-decision procedure.** Since the Single European Act (1986), the Parliament has played a greater role in proposing amendments to Commission proposals in certain areas of policy (e.g. the environment). The co-decision procedure does not give the Parliament power to reject proposals outright or to force its amendments through. It does, however, give MEPs the right to send proposals back to the Council of Ministers for further consideration, making it difficult for the Council to reject changes that also have the approval of the European Commission.

Where does power lie within the Union? Is there a 'democratic deficit'?

The term **'democratic deficit'** refers to a situation where those institutions with the **greatest** democratic mandate have the least power.

Under the Treaty of Rome (1957), most power within the EEC was vested in institutions such as the Commission and the Council of Ministers, rather than the European Parliament.

As the European Parliament remains the only directly elected EU institution, those on the left have argued that it possesses a better mandate to legislate than the Council of Ministers, whose members are normally elected politicians in their own countries but who are not directly elected to the Council of Ministers, or the Commission, whose members are political appointees. Neither of these bodies are directly democratically accountable to European citizens, even though they retain enormous power over them.

Critics of the EU argue that this democratic deficit persists, even though the powers of the European Parliament have been extended in recent years through the co-decision procedure.

Challenging the democratic deficit

Though those on the left criticise the EU for suffering from democratic deficit, those on the right are reluctant to grant the European Parliament more power for fear of taking power out of the hands of member states, and thereby moving towards a *de facto* United States of Europe.

The impact of EU institutions on the Westminster Parliament

UK membership of the EEC — more recently the EU — raises serious questions regarding the UK's **national sovereignty**, i.e. the government's ability to act freely in the best interests of the nation. It is also said to have undermined the **sovereignty**

of Parliament. As we saw earlier in this guide, the incorporation of the Treaty of Rome (1957) into UK law under the European Communities Act (1972) has given EU law preeminence over UK statute, a reality underlined by the *Factortame* case (1990).

When the UK joined the EEC its activities were confined largely to the economic arena, and the UK, as one of nine member states, retained a **national veto** in most significant areas of policy. This is no longer the case:

- The EU is now involved in a far wider **range** of policy areas than was the case when the UK joined the EEC.
- The **enlargement** of the EU from 9 to 27 members (29 from January 2009) has lessened the UK's voice.
- The introduction and extension of **qualified majority voting** to accompany this enlargement has seen the loss of the UK's national veto in most areas of policy.

Questions
&
Answers

This section of the guide looks at a range of answers to the kinds of questions you may face in your Unit 2 examination. It is divided into the four content areas identified in the specification: the British constitution; Parliament; the core executive; and multi-level governance.

For each of these four areas, there is a typical three-part (45-minute) AS question. Each question is accompanied by two model answers: one of A-grade standard and the other of C-grade standard. None of the answers given here is intended to be perfect. Each simply represents one way of approaching the question given, with an indication of the grade that it might achieve.

Immediately after each question, before the student answer, you will find a brief 'examiner's advice' section, which outlines the focus and scope of the question. Following each answer there is an 'examiner's comment' (indicated by the symbol *e*), dealing with the main plus-points and minus-points of the answer. You will also find shorter examiner's comments interspersed throughout the answers. Read all of the examiner's advice and comments sections carefully. They will give you an idea of what you need to do in order to get an A-grade equivalent mark for the question or sub-question. The commentaries will also help you to become more familiar with the three assessment objectives given in the Introduction to this guide.

As is the case with any study aid, this book is aimed at helping you to develop your work — rather than helping you to avoid it! It is far better for you to attempt the questions provided here without first reading the student answers given. Once you have done this you can then review your work in light of the examiner's advice and comments provided. Remember that these student answers are *not* model answers for you to learn and reproduce word-for-word in the examination. It is unlikely that the questions in the examination will be worded exactly as they are here and, in any case, there is always more than one way of answering any question.

The British constitution

Read the extract below and answer parts (a) to (c) which follow.

The nature of the UK constitution

A constitution is an authoritative set of laws, rules and practices specifying how a state is to be governed and the relationship between the state and the individual. The UK constitution is often described as 'unwritten', as no single constitutional document exists. In fact, the UK is best described as having an uncodified constitution. This is because, although there is no single authoritative constitutional document, most of the sources of the UK constitution are written in the form of statute law, case law (common law), European treaties and works of authority.

This loose style of constitution contrasts sharply with that present in most other liberal democracies, such as the USA, though it is important not to underestimate the role that unwritten *conventions* play on both sides of the Atlantic.

Source: adapted from Mark Garnett and Philip Lynch, *UK Government & Politics*
(Philip Allan Updates, 2005)

(a) Explain the term 'conventions' used in the extract. (5 marks)

(b) Using your own knowledge as well as the extract, identify and explain two ways in which constitutional change can be achieved in the UK. (10 marks)

(c) 'The UK would benefit greatly from the introduction of a fully codified constitution.' Discuss. (25 marks)

(a) You should define conventions as those accepted practices or traditions that contribute to the UK's constitutional framework. It would be helpful to give an example of a constitutional convention. You should also comment on the status of such conventions in relation to the other sources of the UK constitution.

(b) A secure understanding of how the UK constitution can be changed will necessarily be rooted in an awareness of constitutional sources. You should focus on the uncodified (from the extract) and unentrenched (from your knowledge) nature of the UK constitution, before focusing on two methods of change, e.g. passing a parliamentary statute, the development of new conventions, judicial action (common law).

(c) To answer this question you will need a good understanding of terms such as 'codified' and 'uncodified'. You should also address the associated notions of 'flexibility' and 'rigidity'. This should then prove a relatively straightforward question. You can either present the main arguments 'for' and 'against' in turn, or organise the various arguments around three themes (e.g. protecting rights, limiting the executive, responding to emergencies).

question

■ ■ ■

A-grade answer

(a) Conventions are established practices — the ways in which things have tradition-ally been done. Although they don't have the legal status of statute law, conven-tions provide a key source of the UK constitution. It is by convention that a lost vote of confidence in the Commons results in a general election. The transfer of royal prerogative powers to the prime minister has also been achieved largely through convention.

> A precise definition, with good examples and recognition that while conventions have little legal force, they are still important. **Full marks.**

(b) As the extract says, statute law is a major source of the UK constitution. In fact, it is the supreme source. Under the doctrine of parliamentary sovereignty, Parliament can make or unmake any law — and no Parliament can bind its succes-sors. Therefore, the easiest way to bring about a constitutional change is by passing an Act of Parliament. Many major constitutional changes have been brought about in this way.

The Parliament Acts (1911 and 1949) altered the relationship between the Commons and the Lords and the House of Lords Act (1999) removed the right of all but 92 hereditary peers to sit and vote in the second chamber. Statute law has also been used to extend the rights of citizens. The Human Rights Act (1998) incor-porated the European Convention on Human Rights into UK law and the Representation of the Peoples Act (1969) reduced the voting age from 21 to 18 years.

A second way in which the constitution can change is through the actions of judges. When members of the Appeals Court and above rule on areas of contro-versy or confusion arising from the law, they can set a legal precedent. This 'judge-made-law' — or common law (case law) — then effectively becomes part of the legal framework. Where their rulings affect the relationships between the govern-ment and the people — or between different parts of government — this will amount to constitutional change. The Donahue vs Stephenson case, for example, extended the rights of consumers by clarifying the nature of criminal responsibility.

> The candidate gives a clear outline of two methods of bringing about constitutional change. Good examples are given throughout, though the case law examples could perhaps have been chosen to have more obvious and far-reaching constitutional implications. A **top A-grade** answer.

(c) A constitution is a set of rules establishing the relationship between the state and its citizens, and between different institutions that comprise the state. In most modern states this set of rules is contained in a single, authoritative document. Codified constitutions of this type are often the product of revolution or newly found independence. The UK, however, is fairly unusual in that it has an uncodified constitution. The rules establishing proper political practice and individual rights in the UK are not written down in a single document but are instead drawn from a number of different sources — some written and some unwritten.

Though uncodified constitutions of the type present in the UK are said to have some clear advantages over the more entrenched codified documents found in other countries — not least the fact that they can be easily changed — they also have their weaknesses. Groups such as Charter 88 have long campaigned for a new, properly codified constitutional settlement for the UK. What would be the positives and the negatives of such a change?

In terms of defining the powers available to various government institutions and establishing the proper relationship between them, a codified constitution for the UK would be a positive move. Such a document would provide greater clarity and transparency. It would allow citizens to clearly see who does what and thereby make it easier for them to hold politicians accountable for their actions. The downside might be that setting relationships in stone in this way might make the system less flexible and adaptable to change. This is often a problem in the USA, where the provisions in the US Constitution often result in gridlock.

In terms of protecting rights, codification could be both a blessing and a curse. A properly codified and entrenched bill of rights would obviously provide better protection to citizens than the current Human Rights Act, which can too easily be ignored or derogated in times of 'emergency'. On the other hand, elevating the status of certain rights by including them in a codified constitution might have the effect of making other unwritten rights appear less important. One also has to take care to ensure that the entrenchment of such rights does not tie one's hands in the future. The US Founding Fathers would probably not have expected the Second Amendment to have acquired the significance it now has.

The final point is that a codified constitution would presumably have a superior status to regular statute. This would have two connected consequences. First, it would signal the end of parliamentary sovereignty. Second, it would put the new UK Supreme Court on a par with its US counterpart. Though some would welcome such a development, others do not believe the judiciary should take on this more overtly political role.

Clearly, then, the move to a codified constitution for the UK would have both good and bad results.

🖉 This response would make it into the A-grade band — it would certainly score very highly on communication (AO3). That said, it could be better. Though the structure is fairly good, the introduction should ideally set out the scope of the essay (which ought to be three or four areas). A proper conclusion would also help. **Low A grade.**

question

C-grade answer

(a) The powers and roles of the cabinet and the prime minister are mostly based in convention. They are not written out clearly in any statute law or in a codified constitution. But conventions can change over time. They are not fixed.

> The candidate gives no real definition or explicit reference to the extract, but the good illustrative examples suggest that the candidate understands the term. **Mid C grade.**

(b) A good deal of the UK constitution is based upon conventions, traditional practices that have developed and become accepted over a number of years. One way in which the constitution can change, therefore, is as a result of changing practices. A good example of this would be the relationship between the prime minister and the cabinet. It was once an accepted convention that cabinet was the place where all of the major decisions were taken. By convention, cabinet was a collective decision-making body bound by another convention, the doctrine of collective responsibility. Over time, however, the role of the prime minister has expanded and these conventions have fallen into disuse.

Another way of changing the UK constitution is by passing a law, e.g. the Freedom of Information Act (2000).

> This answer starts reasonably well. The discussion on conventions is focused, accurate and supported with an appropriate example. Sadly, the second factor is not dealt with in nearly enough detail. **Top C grade.**

(c) The UK would certainly benefit a great deal from the introduction of a fully codified constitution. It would be a positive move in terms of individual rights, scrutiny of the executive, and checks and balances.

Countries with codified constitutions generally offer their citizens better protection of individual rights and freedoms. This is for two reasons. First, such constitutions normally include an integral 'bill of rights'. Second, they are normally entrenched, making it difficult for governments to encroach upon those rights set out simply by passing regular statute. The UK courts would find it far easier to protect individual liberties if they had a superior, codified document they could use to strike down offending Acts of Parliament.

The second good thing about codified constitutions is that they normally provide for more effective checks on the executive. In the UK our system has evolved over time. The prime minister as a result is drawn from Parliament and exercises the prerogative powers once held by the hereditary monarch. This results in executive dominance or elective dictatorship. A properly codified constitution would clearly set out both the powers of the various government institutions and the limitations acting upon them.

This takes me on to my third point, that there would be better checks and balances like in the USA, where presidents cannot do much at all without the approval of one or both houses of Congress.

This is a fairly focused response, but it has a number of weaknesses. First, it is completely one-sided. There is no attempt to consider the view that codification might be a bad thing for the UK. Second, in one of these longer 25-mark questions, an examiner would ideally be looking for three developed points. In this case the third point is not sufficiently distinct from the second one. Third, the candidate clearly runs out of time and is therefore unable to draw the answer together with a proper conclusion. **Mid C grade**.

Parliament

Read the extract below and answer parts (a) to (c) which follow.

The passage of legislation

(1) The Queen's speech: once it has been agreed among cabinet members, the government's legislative programme is announced at the beginning of each parliamentary session in the Queen's speech.

(2) First reading: the formal announcement that a bill is to be introduced. No Commons vote.

(3) Second reading: the key stage, where MPs debate the principle of the bill. Followed by a vote.

(4) Committee stage: Once it has passed its second reading the bill is allotted to the relevant standing committee. Each line of the bill is scrutinised at this stage and changes can be recommended.

(5) Third reading: bills cannot be amended at this stage (except in the Lords). They have to be accepted or rejected as a whole. This means that there are fewer debates and votes.

(6) House of Lords: each bill has to negotiate a similar obstacle course in the Lords. The upper house can offer its own amendments to the bill, though it no longer has the right to reject legislation as a result of the Parliament Acts (1911 and 1949).

(7) Royal Assent: necessary for a bill to pass into law, though simply a formality; no monarch has refused to sign legislation since Queen Anne in 1707.

Source: adapted from Mark Garnett and Philip Lynch, *UK Government & Politics*
(Philip Allan Updates, 2005)

(a) **Explain the term 'the Parliament Acts' used in the extract.** (5 marks)

(b) **Using your own knowledge as well as the extract, examine the part that standing committees play in the legislative process.** (10 marks)

(c) **'Transforming the House of Lords into a fully elected second chamber would create more problems than it would solve.' Assess the accuracy of this view.** (25 marks)

(a) When defining the term 'the Parliament Acts' you will need to explain precisely what powers these Acts afford the Commons in their dealings with the Lords. Although it is not necessary to demonstrate an awareness of *why* the 1911 Act was passed, offering an example from your own knowledge of it being used would make you more likely to achieve the higher levels on the mark scheme.

(b) The extract states that such committees consider legislation after the second reading in the Commons, scrutinising bills and suggesting amendments. You could use your own knowledge to comment on the ad hoc nature of these committees, their relative lack of power, and the extent to which the whips control their activities.

(c) It would be helpful to demonstrate an awareness of 'where we are' in terms of House of Lords reform (following the 1999 House of Lords Act) and why Lords reform is even on the agenda — i.e. identify the 'problems' with the current arrangements in the upper chamber. This will provide a framework for assessing whether a fully elected chamber would cause more problems than it would solve.

■ ■ ■

A-grade answer

(a) The Parliament Acts give the House of Commons the ultimate power to force legislation through the Lords. In effect the Lords can now only delay non-money bills for a year and they cannot do a great deal at all to money bills such as the Budget. The 1911 Parliament Act was passed following the budget crisis of 1909, when the unelected Lords tried to block the Budget put forward by the elected government. The Parliament Act hasn't actually been used that often. It was used to force the Hunting Act through in 2004.

A solid definition, demonstrating awareness of what the Act does, and an example. **Full marks**.

(b) UK standing committees play a crucial role in the passage of legislation. A bill is normally sent to a standing committee following its second reading in the Commons. The role of the committee is, as outlined in the extract, to scrutinise the bill clause by clause, correcting clerical errors and recommending amendments to Parliament. Though committees do not really play a role in discussing the principle of the bill in question — that is done at second reading — they can recommend significant changes, particularly when the law has been hurriedly and/or badly drafted.

Although standing committees play an important role, however, they are relatively insignificant when compared to their US counterparts. UK standing committees are ad hoc rather than permanent. This is not the case in many other democracies, where committee members often spend decades on a single committee and gain great knowledge and expertise within a particular area of policy. UK standing committees are also short on resources and they are denied the legal right to subpoena witnesses and evidence as part of their investigation into the merits of the legislation. Finally, the composition of a standing committee reflects that of the House of Commons. This means that the majority party in the Commons (i.e. the government) can normally get what it wants out of a committee through the use of its whips.

✐ This is an excellent answer in terms of knowledge and understanding. The candidate clearly understands the theoretical role of such committees as well as some of the criticisms commonly levelled at them. One or two precise examples would have taken this to the top of the A grade. **Mid A grade.**

(c) When New Labour was returned to office in 1997, following 18 years in opposition, it came with a manifesto commitment to reform the House of Lords. The upper chamber it had faced in the late 1990s, like the one it faced when last in government in the late 1970s, had an inbuilt Tory majority, with 471 Conservative peers to Labour's 179. Many of these members were hereditary peers (over 750 of the 1,300 Lords). The party therefore had two good reasons for wanting to reform the Lords: first, because it was likely to present a significant obstacle to Labour's radical agenda; and second, because the hereditary principle appeared indefensible as the country prepared for the twenty-first century.

However, things have changed since 1997. The House of Lords Act (1999) removed the right of all but 92 of the 750 hereditary peers to sit and vote in the House of Lords, and by May 2008 Labour peers actually outnumbered Conservative peers by 217 to 202. In addition, many regard the part-reformed chamber created in 1999 as the most effective second chamber in memory. This does raise the question of whether moving to an entirely elected chamber would actually make things any better.

The first problem in creating an entirely elected Lords is precisely what would happen to the existing peers. It could be argued that those currently serving in the chamber probably have considerably more life experience and wisdom than those elected to the Commons. Losing such enormous experience would surely make Parliament a worse place. Though this problem could be overcome by phasing elections in over a number of years, as was suggested in the 2007 White Paper, there are other problems with moving to a fully elected model.

The pre-eminence of the Commons, and the convention that governments are largely drawn from the lower house, both result from the fact that it is the elected chamber. This was recognised with the passage of the Parliament Acts of 1911 and 1949. If we moved towards a totally elected Lords, the new chamber might easily claim its own electoral mandate, i.e. in opposition to that of the Commons. Any move towards an elected Lords should properly involve a separate election for the executive, therefore.

The third problem is that a Lords elected at the same time as the Commons and, presumably, having a similar party composition, would not be as effective a check on the Commons as is the current Lords. The fact that the Lords has been a 'hung' chamber since 1999 and is likely to remain so means that it is remarkably independent of mind — and this is helped by the fact that peers don't have to be elected.

The 2007 White Paper on Lords reform managed to work its way around all of these problems by a variety of means, e.g. guaranteeing the Commons supremacy, having Lords elections at different times, only allowing Lords to serve a single term (thus removing the need for them to pander to voters). At the end of the day, however, one must question whether such a compromised chamber would be any better than what we have at present.

🖉 This is a nicely argued answer. The introductory section starts off in an overly descriptive style, but the essay is well on track by the second paragraph. Specific examples of the Lords in action would have helped to support some of the points made. **Mid A grade.**

C-grade answer

(a) The Parliament Acts let the Commons force legislation through the Lords, because they are the elected chamber. There were two Acts, the first in 1911 and the second in 1949. It isn't used that often.

🖉 This answer is focused, but little more than an outline. The definition needs more development and the answer should include an example. **Low C grade.**

(b) There are two main types of committee in the House of Commons. Departmental select committees originated in the 1970s. They perform a scrutiny function, checking the work of government departments and holding the executive to account. Though select committees have been criticised for lacking power ('watchdogs with no teeth'), they can cause the government real embarrassment. The late Gwyneth Dunwoody, chair of the transport select committee, was a thorn in the side of government. The Labour Party even tried to use its influence on the committee to secure the election of a more 'New Labour' chair, but it failed.

There are also some non-departmental select committees, such as the Public Accounts Committee (PAC). This works across the full range of government activity, checking for financial efficiency. The PAC has exposed numerous examples of poor financial management.

The second main kind of committee is standing committees. These committees have the role of scrutinising legislation, as the extract says, spotting any typos and making amendments. In reality, standing committees rarely make major changes to bills that come before them, because they are dominated by the party which controls the Commons.

🖉 The first two paragraphs of this answer lack focus. It is all too easy to slip into a pre-learnt response on Commons committees, without focusing on what the question is asking you (in this case, about standing committees only). This candidate wastes a considerable amount of time dealing with select committees and this material is simply not creditable — however good it is — in answer to this question. A **D-grade** response.

(c) It is quite ridiculous that we should still have an entirely unelected second chamber in the twenty-first century. It is simply crazy for the government to keep giving MPs and peers a free vote on multiple-option proposals when they were prepared to use up over 700 hours of parliamentary time and the Parliament Act to force through the Hunting Act.

Under the resemblance theory of representation, legislators and those in high public office should be broadly representative of those they serve. The Lords will never resemble the broader public as long as it is a wholly appointed chamber. Moving towards a fully elected second chamber will bring us into line with virtually every other bicameral legislature around the world. It will make members of the chamber directly accountable to the people, a key feature of any so-called democracy, and thereby enhance representation. It will also extend opportunities for political participation because the public will have more people they can elect and more people they can target when lobbying in pursuit of a particular cause.

On the other hand, is the Lords really that bad? Back in the early 1990s the *News of the World* ran with the headline, 'Oh Lord what a load of lazy layabouts', but things have changed a lot since then. Most of the hereditary peers have now gone and most of those who remain are making an excellent contribution to government. The risk of turning the Lords into another elected chamber would be that we just end up with 600 more career politicians who are more interested in lining their own pockets than they are in doing their best for the people of Britain!

🖉 Not a great opening paragraph. You should ideally write in a more measured, academic style and avoid value judgements — particularly ones which effectively conclude — in your introduction. Though there are some good analytical points in paragraphs two and three, the essay is overly polemical and lacking in depth. **Low C grade**.

Question 3

The core executive

Read the extract below and answer parts (a) to (c) which follow.

Relations within the core executive

Martin J. Smith argued that those who focus entirely on the relationship between prime minister and cabinet do so because they believe that power relationships within the core executive are based upon 'command', whereas they are in fact rooted in mutual 'dependence'. Power is fragmented and progress is possible only when a sufficient number of players are brought onboard. If one accepts this view, then the prime minister becomes less of a 'presidential' figure and more of a 'line manager'; assigning roles and responsibilities, managing rivalries among his middle managers, and trying to ensure that the bureaucratic 'tail' doesn't 'wag the dog'.

In its efforts to allow this kind of managerial control, New Labour brought massive changes to the core executive during its first 10 years in office. It reworked the Cabinet Office, developed the Prime Minister's Office, made greater use of special advisers, and moved key individuals closer to the prime minister by giving them offices in Downing Street.

Source: adapted from Paul Fairclough, *The Prime Minister & the Cabinet* (Philip Allan Updates, 2007)

(a) **Explain the term 'Cabinet Office' used in this extract.** (5 marks)

(b) **Using your own knowledge as well as the extract, identify and explain two ways in which the core executive has changed since 1997.** (10 marks)

(c) **'The office of the prime minister is what its holder chooses and is able to make of it.' Discuss.** (25 marks)

(a) The extract identifies the Cabinet Office (CO) as a key element of the core executive, noting that the body has been 'reworked' in recent years. To achieve a reasonable mark on this question, you will need to move beyond this material by setting out precisely what the CO *is* and what it *does*. At the very least you should mention the cabinet secretary, the various secretariats and the roles the CO performs.

(b) The extract describes the reorganisation of the Cabinet Office and the Prime Minister's Office in recent years and the extent to which such bodies have been brought closer to the prime minister — both physically and in terms of line management. You could use your own knowledge to develop this point (e.g. by referring to the emergence of a virtual 'Prime Minister's Department') or to make additional points (e.g. the much-heralded decline of the cabinet as a collective decision-making body).

(c) This question focuses on the power of the prime minister. The quotation in the title, from Herbert Asquith, suggests that the potential for power is always present in the office of prime minister, but that it is the abilities of the incumbent which determine the extent to which this potential is realised. You could simply present the arguments 'for' and 'against' this view. Alternatively, you could look at a number of variables which might determine the power of the prime minister, e.g. the incumbent's abilities, the abilities of those around them (in the government and in opposition), or the political context (size of Commons majority, 'Events, dear boy. Events' etc.).

■ ■ ■

A-grade answer

(a) The Cabinet Office was founded in 1916 as a body that could properly coordinate the work of the various government departments in times of war. Though it was once merely a bureaucratic body, consisting of a number of secretariats, the modern Cabinet Office comprises over twenty separate units (e.g. the Better Regulation Executive) and plays a vital role in coordinating government activity. Some see the growth of the Cabinet Office and the parallel growth of the Prime Minister's Office under New Labour as tantamount to the creation of a Prime Minister's Department.

> ✏ This response is very good in terms of definition and gives some excellent factual knowledge in support. The candidate has certainly done enough to gain an **A grade**, but the answer could be stronger on roles and should ideally mention the cabinet secretary.

(b) The core executive has undergone a massive transformation since 1997. According to the extract, New Labour reorganised the Cabinet Office and the Prime Minister's Office, as well as making greater use of special advisers in its efforts to 'allow this kind of managerial control'.

The first big area of change has been in the Cabinet Office (CO). Whereas the CO was once seen as a largely bureaucratic body consisting of a number of secretariats, it has been transformed under New Labour into a real engine house of the cabinet system. Although the various formal secretariats still play an important role in coordinating the work of government departments, a whole range of new bodies, such as the Prime Minister's Delivery Unit and the Strategy Unit, have brought the CO into the policy-making arena.

The Prime Minister's Office has also expanded massively over the same period, both with the creation of new bodies such as the Policy Directorate and with the emergence of a number of key positions — not least the role of prime minister's chief of staff. At the same time, the Prime Minister's Office and the Cabinet Office have become merged to the extent that many writers now feel they constitute a Prime Minister's Department in all but name. For example, the Strategy Unit is in the Cabinet Office but the Head of the Strategy Unit also works in the Prime Minister's Office.

All of these changes, and the increasing reliance upon special advisers, reflect the deep distrust with which New Labour viewed the regular civil service when it returned to office in 1997. New Labour was determined that the service would not obstruct its radical agenda in the same way that Labour governments in the 1960s and 1970s had often been frustrated.

> ⌨ This is certainly an A-grade response, though it is rather narrow in scope. A more balanced answer might, for example, consider the changing relationship between the prime minister and cabinet during this period, as both are elements of the core executive.

(c) The powers of the prime minister have developed largely through convention. There is no centrally codified and entrenched list of precisely what the incumbent may or may not do. As a result, Asquith was probably right to conclude that 'the office of the prime minister is what its holder chooses and is able to make of it' — or to put it another way, the PM has the power to do whatever he can 'get away with'.

However, if we look more closely at Asquith's remark we can see that things are not quite as clear as they might appear at first. This is because whether or not the incumbent is 'able' to do something will depend as much upon the abilities of those around him, and on circumstance, as it does upon the prime minister's abilities. We can see this quite clearly when looking at the case of Gordon Brown.

In terms of his personal abilities, Brown clearly has some of the skills that are required of the modern prime minister. He is unquestionably capable intellectually and he enjoyed an impressive track record as chancellor of the exchequer during New Labour's first decade in office. However, in other respects, Gordon Brown was found wanting in the wake of his move to Number 10. First, he is less comfortable in the media spotlight than his predecessor, Tony Blair. Brown's performances at Prime Minister's Questions have brought criticism and commentators have also questioned his political instincts, e.g. over the general election that wasn't in the autumn of 2007. Although he has clearly 'chosen' his path as prime minister, there are some question marks over whether or not he is 'able' to carry it off.

The second variable concerns the abilities of those around the incumbent prime minister. Though Brown was unchallenged as Labour leader when Blair stood down in 2007, this was clearly not a sign that the entire parliamentary party was totally behind the chancellor. Indeed, many of those who might have stood against Brown either lacked the experience in government or the backbench support necessary to sustain a worthwhile challenge. The emergence of figures such as Ed Balls and David Miliband since 2007 means that there are now 'able' alternatives to whom backbenchers might lend support should things turn sour. In

question

addition, Brown is now facing far more able opposition from outside of government, not least in the person of the Conservative leader David Cameron. Brown would surely have been more 'able' to impose his will were Michael Howard still leader of the official opposition.

The third and final variable is that of circumstance or, as Harold Macmillan put it, 'Events, dear boy. Events'. Regardless of the incumbent prime minister's abilities and the abilities of those around him or her, events clearly have the capacity to make the task of imposing one's will either a good deal easier, or virtually impossible. Brown has had to contend with the ongoing situation in Iraq and Afghanistan — wars that did for his predecessor, despite his media savvy. Brown's premiership was also damaged by the Northern Rock fiasco, the 'global credit crunch' and the row over the '10p-in-the-pound' tax rate. Such events, coupled to bad results in local elections and in the Crewe and Nantwich by-election, inevitably result in disquiet on the backbenches — particularly when a general election is less than 2 years away.

In short, prime ministerial power is not simply about whether or not the prime minister has the necessary personal abilities or qualities to do the job. The extent to which he is able to assert himself will also be affected by the abilities of others, events, or even the sense that it is 'time for a change'.

✍ This is an excellent answer. Rather than just rolling out a pre-prepared response on 'the power of the prime minister', this candidate has got to grips with the quotation and structured a response accordingly. **Top A grade.**

C-grade answer

(a) The Cabinet Office is part of the core executive. It organises the cabinet's paperwork, e.g. agendas and minutes. The cabinet secretary is in charge of the Cabinet Office. It is supposed to help 'joined-up government'.

✍ This answer is fairly solid in terms of the role of the Cabinet Office. The candidate shows some good knowledge (e.g. the role of the cabinet secretary), but is more limited on what the Cabinet Office actually consists of. **Borderline B/C grade.**

(b) The main elements of the core executive are the prime minister and the cabinet. In this sense, the core executive has changed dramatically since 1997. The main way in which things have changed is in terms of the relationship between the prime minister and the cabinet. Traditionally the cabinet was supposed to be at the heart of government. It was, as Bagehot said, a buckle that joined the executive part of the government to the legislature. Bagehot said that cabinet was the efficient secret of the English constitution; the place where real power resided.

Since 1997, however, all of this has changed. Blair placed far less emphasis on cabinet, preferring instead to rely upon other individuals within the core executive — such as the Cabinet Office, the Prime Minister's Office and special advisers (all mentioned in the extract). Blair took big decisions outside of cabinet (e.g. the

Millennium Dome) and turned cabinet into little more than a talking shop. Mo Mowlam said that cabinet government is dead. That is the biggest change in the core executive since 1997.

🖉 This response is quite focused, although the candidate is clearly trying to turn the question into one on the relationship between the prime minister and cabinet. The second paragraph gets things back on track, but there is far too little depth on precisely how the core executive has changed. **B/C-grade borderline**.

(c) The power of the UK prime minister can be divided into five broad areas: powers of patronage; powers over cabinet, government and the civil service; powers over Parliament; powers over the political agenda and policy; and powers on the world stage.

The prime minister has considerable powers of patronage. By convention, the prime minister appoints members of the cabinet and other ministers on behalf the monarch. He also appoints heads of nationalised industries, leading figures in the civil service, peers, and senior bishops in the Church of England. Such powers of patronage give the prime minister the opportunity to shape the government as he sees fit. In the case of ministerial positions, the prime minister has the power to 'fire' in addition to his power to 'hire'.

The prime minister has considerable powers within the executive, beyond his power to appoint leading figures. He sets the agenda in cabinet and controls the flow of meetings, should he choose to take decisions in cabinet at all. He also controls the network of cabinet committees and decides who chairs each committee. In recent years, leading civil servants have become far more directly accountable to the prime minister.

As the leader of the majority party in the Commons, the prime minister has the power to set the political agenda by ensuring that his proposals are given the lion's share of the time available in Parliament. Through his control of the party whips, the prime minister can normally ensure that the measures he favours get safe passage through the Commons.

The final area of prime ministerial power is that which comes as a result of the role the modern premier plays on the world stage. Having by convention assimilated most of the royal prerogative powers, the prime minister is the leading UK figure abroad — far more so than the foreign secretary. The prime minister's power to make war and conclude treaties is central to this role.

🖉 This is a reasonable survey of the powers of the prime minister, though it is somewhat lacking in terms of precise examples. In addition, the candidate makes little attempt to address the terms of the question directly (i.e. by not giving any explicit reference to the quotation). **Top C grade**.

Q4

Multi-level governance

Read the extract below and answer parts (a) to (c) which follow.

New Labour's devolution programme

Labour's huge parliamentary majority and the referendum 'yes' votes ensured a relatively smooth passage for the bills establishing devolved institutions in Scotland and Wales. They began their work after the first elections to the new bodies were held in May 1999.

Devolution has been asymmetric. Rather than following a standard blueprint, each of the devolved institutions has different powers and distinctive features. The Scottish Parliament has primary legislative powers (the power to make laws) and tax-raising powers. The Welsh Assembly is weaker, having only executive powers — the power to implement laws made at Westminster or to issue secondary legislation within the existing legal framework.

The creation of such devolved institutions has proven controversial, not least because both Scotland and Wales still send MPs to the Westminster Parliament.

Source: adapted from Mark Garnett & Philip Lynch, *UK Government & Politics*
(Philip Allan Updates, 2005)

(a) **Explain the term 'primary legislative powers' used in the extract.** (5 marks)

(b) **Using your own knowledge as well as the extract, explain why the creation of the Scottish Parliament and the Welsh Assembly has proven controversial.** (10 marks)

(c) **'Essentially the UK is now a federal as opposed to a unitary state.' Discuss.** (25 marks)

(a) You should define the term as the ability to make laws independently of the Westminster Parliament. Ideally you should identify the areas of policy within which the devolved institutions in Scotland hold this power (with a specific example) and contrast such primary legislative powers with the weaker secondary legislative or administrative powers granted to the Welsh Assembly.

(b) The extract makes the closing point that devolution has proven controversial because both Scotland and Wales still send MPs to Westminster. You could use your own knowledge to develop this point, e.g. by referring to the West Lothian Question. More specifically, it would be relevant to mention some of those Commons votes on devolved issues which were only passed with the support of MPs representing non-English constituencies, e.g. on university top-up fees and foundation hospitals. You could link this point to calls for an English Parliament, or 'English votes for English laws'.

(c) To answer this question you will need to demonstrate a good theoretical under-standing of the fundamental differences between unitary and federal states. You will also need to be able to apply this theoretical knowledge to developments in the UK since 1997. Better responses will draw a distinction between how things are legally and constitutionally (i.e. still unitary) and how they look to the average citizen (i.e. increasingly federal). It would be helpful to consider the integration of the UK within the EU as well as the process of devolving power down from Westminster.

■ ■ ■

A-grade answer

(a) The primary legislative powers given to the devolved institutions in Scotland are more extensive than those given to the Welsh Assembly. The Scottish Parliament is free to make laws as it sees fit within those areas placed under devolved control in the 1990s. It does not have to ask permission from Westminster before making such laws, e.g. the decision not to introduce university top-up fees or foundation hospitals. The devolved institutions in Wales only have administrative or secondary legislative powers. This means that in theory the Westminster Parliament has to OK everything that they do.

> ☑ The candidate gives a solid definition, supported by examples. Though the comments regarding the power of devolved institutions in Wales could be a little more precise, he/she clearly understands the fundamental difference between primary legislative powers and administrative powers. A good **A-grade** response.

(b) The UK has traditionally been said to be a unitary state. Ultimate power and authority is held by the central government, and ultimately by Parliament at Westminster. Linked into this is the doctrine of parliamentary sovereignty, the notion that Parliament can make or unmake any law and that only Parliament can make law. This then is the first reason why devolution to Scotland and Wales has proven controversial. If indeed we are a unitary state, why should major decisions affecting the lives of people in Scotland — and to a lesser extent Wales — be taken anywhere other than at Westminster?

The second reason why devolution has proven controversial links power with representation in the form of the 'West Lothian Question'. This question, first posed by Labour MP Tam Dalyell, raised the issue of what would happen once powers over areas such as healthcare were devolved to Scotland, yet MPs representing Scottish constituencies would — as it says in the extract — still be sitting in Westminster, voting on bills that would only affect those in England or in England and Wales. This issue of over- (for the Scots) or under- (for the English) represen-tation is a key reason why devolution to Scotland and Wales has proven contro-versial and why some in England now call for an English Parliament — or English votes for English laws at Westminster. The fact that the Scottish institutions have

4

primary legislative powers, as the extract notes, makes devolution to Scotland more contentious than that to Wales.

The third reason why such changes have proven controversial is because of what the Scots and the Welsh have actually done with the powers granted. In the case of Scotland, for example, the devolved institutions have provided free nursing care for the elderly and opted not to introduce university top-up fees or foundation hospitals. Many people in England resent the Scots getting what are widely seen as 'better' policies when English taxpayers are still subsidising those in Scotland by over £2,000 per capita, per annum.

> *This is a top **A-grade** answer. The candidate identifies a number of reasons why devolution has proven controversial and develops each point using his/her own knowledge.*

(c) The UK is generally referred to as being a unitary state as opposed to a federal one. Under a unitary system of government, the ultimate power and authority within a state is held at central government level. Any power that local government or regional government appears to have is merely delegated or 'devolved' to it and can be withdrawn at any time. In the UK context, this means that real power is, in theory at least, held by the central government at Westminster. Although the Scottish Parliament, the Welsh Assembly and other sub-national government (e.g. local government) may appear to have varying degrees of power, they are all subject to the same central authority: the UK Parliament.

Under a federal system, in contrast, supreme power is divided between a central government and a number of regions or individual states. Each tier of government has ultimate authority over certain areas of policy — which means that they have separate jurisdictions. Because the relationship between the central government and the states or regions that make up the nation is normally fixed and entrenched, it is impossible for the central government to abolish these states or to significantly reduce their power without their consent.

Although the UK is, in theory, still as unitary a state as it ever was, a number of developments since the 1970s have led some to suggest that the UK is moving towards something more akin to a federal model. Of these developments, it is the programme of devolution that New Labour pursued after 1997 that has resulted in the greatest debate. The question over precisely 'how federal' the UK system has become has been particularly focused on the devolved institutions in Scotland. These bodies are fundamentally different to those in Wales, because whereas the Welsh institutions were simply given administrative or secondary legislative powers, the Scottish Parliament was given primary legislative powers in a wide range of areas, as well as the ability to vary the rate of taxation. This means that the Scottish Parliament is effectively free to act as it sees fit in areas such as education and healthcare, e.g. the decision not to introduce university top-up fees or foundation hospitals. In fact, the devolved institutions in Scotland now have powers not wholly dissimilar from those commonly held by states or regions within a federal system.

European integration since our entry into the EEC in 1973 has also raised the possibility that the UK is moving towards a federal system, though this time with the UK as the middle tier of government under the EU and above regional government. With the EU now having branched out into policy areas not even considered at the time of our entry into the community, one could question the extent to which the UK central government is still the single central authority governing the UK. This is particularly true when one considers the extension of qualified majority voting into most areas of European policy. The UK no longer has a national veto on most decisions.

While all of this is true, however, the fact remains that the Westminster Parliament can always withdraw powers that have been devolved or delegated as it sees fit. Though the central government might feel morally obliged to hold a further referendum before reversing a decision that was authorised by a referendum, it is under no legal obligation to do so. Returning such powers to Westminster would not be an easy option but it is possible, as was seen with the suspension of power-sharing arrangements in Northern Ireland between 2002 and 2007.

> 🖉 This is an excellent response. The candidate clearly has a comprehensive understanding of the nature of unitary and federal systems and is able to assess, with great subtlety, the changes that have taken place in the UK since the 1970s. **Top A grade.**

C-grade answer

(a) When the Scottish Parliament was created it was given more power than many of the other devolved institutions in Wales, etc. This is because Scotland has always had more autonomy in terms of things such as its legal system and education. In Scotland most students take Highers instead of A-levels. The referendum which approved plans for a Scottish Parliament also gave the new body tax-varying powers. The Welsh Assembly was not given this power.

> 🖉 The candidate gives no real definition here, although he/she clearly understands that devolved institutions in Scotland were given more power than their Welsh counterparts. Some good knowledge is shown, but it needs to be deployed in support of a proper definition. **Mid C grade.**

(b) The main reason why devolution to Scotland and Wales has proven controversial is that the Scots and Welsh have effectively been given power to govern themselves even though English taxpayers are still subsidising both nations massively, in part as a result of the Barnett Formula. For example, the vote on top-up fees was only carried at Westminster with the support of MPs from Scottish constituencies. Ironically, even though these MPs' constituents will not have to pay top-up fees, because the Scottish executive has not introduced them north of

the border, Scottish universities will still get extra money under the Barnett Formula. Although they reduced the number of parliamentary constituencies in Scotland from 72 to 59 at the time of the 2005 general election, it is still wrong that an MP (even the prime minister!) should be able to vote on laws that have no bearing at all on their constituents. This is why the Tories want English votes for English laws.

> ✍ There is lots of good content here and some good argument too — but no real sense of structure. The other major fault is that the candidate makes no real reference to or use of the material in the extract. This would limit the mark to a **mid C grade**, at best.

(c) When the Founding Fathers wrote the US Constitution, they were keen to avoid creating an over-powerful central government. In fact, they wanted to create a system of limited government, where the executive, legislature and judiciary were separated at federal level and where power was also divided between the central government and the various states. Under the 10th amendment to the Constitution, ratified in 1791, those powers not delegated to the federal government or denied to the states remain with the states or with the people. This created a proper federal system where each tier of government (federal and state) had its own area of jurisdiction and the powers of the various states could not be taken away without their consent. For example, under the US system of government individual states are free to decide whether or not to have the death penalty, whereas the central (federal) government controls things such as defence.

The UK system is different. Whereas in the USA the federal government was created by the states at the Philadelphia Convention, in the UK power comes from the centre, and any powers that sub-national government appears to have is only really 'on loan' from central government. Crucially, Parliament remains sovereign.

Although this is true in theory, things appear to be rather different in reality. The devolution programme launched by New Labour in 1997 has seen significant powers granted to the Scottish Parliament and the Welsh Assembly. This means that the UK is becoming more federal, as the question suggests. But this power can be taken back by Westminster if it wants to. That is the main difference between a federal and a unitary system. In a federal system the relationship between the various sub-national units of government and the central government is entrenched, whereas in a unitary system supreme power remains at the centre, whatever it might look like 'on the ground'.

> ✍ This candidate clearly understands the issues central to the question but spends far too much time detailing the constitutional arrangements in the USA. Candidates should remember that AS Unit 2 (GOVP2) is *not* a comparative UK/USA unit. Although references to the USA can be credited where they help to illustrate the characteristics of the UK system, there is little to be gained from writing at length

on countries other than the UK. In the case of this answer, the time wasted on the USA could have been spent more productively by dealing with the nature and scope of UK devolution in more depth. **Mid C grade.**